T0063984

JESUS CHRIST

- TRUE MAN, TRUE PROPHET

An Islamic Approach to
Understanding the Scriptures

OMAR W. NOOR

authorHOUSE®

AuthorHouse™
1663 Liberty Drive
Bloomington, IN 47403
www.authorhouse.com
Phone: 1-800-839-8640

Published by AuthorHouse 02/17/2014

ISBN: 978-1-4918-5905-6 (sc)
ISBN: 978-1-4918-5904-9 (e)

Library of Congress Control Number: 2014901882

بِسْمِ اللهِ الرَّحْمٰنِ الرَّحِيْمِ

**In the name of Allah (God),
the beneficent, the merciful**

CONTENTS

PREFACE

Why is a Muslim writing about Jesus? Don't they have their own God?

If you believe that Islam is against Jesus, God, or the Bible, then you are probably not alone. As a Christian growing up in the suburbs of America, I myself was once oblivious to the fact that Jesus is regarded as a prophet in Islam and that *Allah* is essentially the Arabic word for God. I had always assumed that Allah was some foreign god and that Muhammad was to Islam what Jesus is to Christianity. I knew that Muslims had a book called the Koran but could not imagine it being even remotely similar to the Bible.

When I learned about the honor and respect assigned to Jesus in Islam, and that the miracle of his birth is validated in the Koran, I began to realize that Islam and Christianity are connected in a way that reflects the relationship between Judaism and Christianity, and when they told me that Muhammad preached the same message of monotheism as Abraham, Moses, and Jesus, it made sense to me that God, the Creator of us all, would have a universal message that would stand the test of time.

These similarities, or familiarities, if you will, are what attracted me initially to Islam, but then the more I learned about the Muslim faith, the more I found it to be true. Islam seemed to have the answer for everything—even the purpose of life[1]—and what I found most compelling is the inclusion of science in the sacred text of Islam (i.e., the Koran).

But still I had doubts, and what bothered me most is the apparent implication that the Bible could be wrong. If Jesus wasn't God, I thought, then why was he portrayed as such in what is referred to by millions as the word of God. I wanted to be clear and somehow reconcile the sacred scriptures with the Jesus of Islam, and so I began the research that eventually led to the production of this book, and in my humble attempt to unravel the mystery of the Bible, I believe I have uncovered the truth about Jesus.

I hope that you, the reader, will agree, at least, that an objective approach was taken to arrive at this conclusion, and if you find it beneficial, all praise is due to Allah (God).

The subject matter of this document is inherently controversial; however, it is not the intent of the author to ridicule or offend anyone. The idea, rather, is to stimulate debate while educating non-Muslims on the Islamic view of Jesus. The arguments presented here are designed to be straightforward and irrefutable but at the same time

---

[1]   The purpose of life, as defined in the Koran, is to serve God, either willingly or unwillingly, in accordance with His divine plan.

nonconfrontational. The reader is encouraged to approach this material with an open mind and a clean heart, and with the ultimate goal of determining for him/herself what is the truth. May Allah (God) the Exalted guide those who seek the truth.

INTRODUCTION

From the time of Adam to the present age, there is perhaps no man in history whose name is familiar to more people throughout the globe than Jesus of Nazareth, a.k.a. Jesus Christ; nor is one likely to find anyone whose life is filled with more controversy and mystery than the man born to Mary "in the days of Herod."[1] To the Jews he is irrelevant, a contemptuous prophet at best; while to the vast majority of Christians, he is nothing short of the Creator himself. The Muslim view of Jesus, based largely on the Koran, lies squarely in the middle of these two extremes and, as the following document is intended to show, agrees in essence with the spirit of the Bible and what the early evangelists perceived of his nature and origin.

In many ways the Koran is consistent with the Christian view of Jesus and, incidentally, consistent with the Bible in the same regard. The miraculous birth of Jesus,[2] for instance, his ability to perform miracles,[3] his designation

---

[1]   In the Gospel according to Luke, the birth of Jesus is connected to the reign of Herod the Great (circa 40 BC–4 BC).

[2]   See chapter 19, verses 16–22 of the Holy Koran.

[3]   See chapter 3, verse 49 of the Holy Koran.

as the Messiah,[1] and the expectation of his return[2] are all points of agreement firmly established in the Koran. On the issue of divinity, however, the Koran adamantly rejects the notion that Jesus is God.[3]

The belief that Jesus is as much divine as he is human is not only a source of contention between Islam and Christianity; it has long been disputed within the ranks of the Christian community itself, from the second century of the church, when Monarchianism[4] flourished, until more recently, with the formation of various Unitarian sects.

Those who dispute the "orthodox"[5] view of Jesus generally adhere to the same canonical texts as the mainstream Christians sects but do not accept the traditional interpretation of these texts set forth by the so-called "Fathers of the Church." They recognize certain discrepancies between the doctrines and beliefs upheld by the church and the testimony of the early evangelists imbedded in the manuscripts they left behind.

---

[1]   See chapter 3, verse 45 of the Holy Koran.
[2]   See chapter 43, verse 61 of the Holy Koran.
[3]   See chapter 5, verses 17 and 75 of the Holy Koran.
[4]   Monarchianism was an early Christian theology that stressed the oneness of God in opposition to the Trinity.
       The Adoptionists, considered proponents of Monarchianism, even denied the belief that Jesus preexisted.
[5]   The Greek term *orthodox*(os), meaning "pure" or "sound" thinking, was used by the church to differentiate between its own authorized doctrines and those beliefs it deemed heretic.

The doctrines and beliefs upheld by the church were presumably derived from the sacred texts of both the Hebrew Bible and the Christian canon, although many of the essential terms and phrases used to develop these articles of faith, such as the Trinity or original sin, do not appear anywhere in the ancient scriptures. These innovative expressions, however well intentioned, reveal a careless departure from the apostolic tradition reflected in the Bible by later generations, as well as a failure on the part of the church to preserve the message of Jesus.

This is not to say that each of the twenty-seven books that make up the New Testament represent the theological views of the first generation of believers who followed Jesus during the days of his ministry. The authenticity of the Bible is difficult to determine with any level of preciseness, as there is little or no traceability between the extant manuscripts and the original compositions, and in many cases, neither the author nor the time of composition is fully known. The point is that the Bible, as it exists today, authentic or not, contains the oldest written testimony accepted by the church regarding the life and times of Jesus. Therefore, any deviation from these sacred manuscripts by later Christian communities ought to be thoroughly scrutinized.

Throughout history people have been inclined to follow the religion of their parents without ever considering the possibility that, at some point in time, their forefathers might have been led astray by cultural influences or in some other way misguided, which is certainly understandable, however, not entirely rational. For those who believe in God and a day of reckoning, religion is arguably the most important facet of human life, because it is our relationship with God that ultimately determines our fate in the Hereafter. It is imperative, therefore, for those who truly believe in God and fear him, to examine their faith and assure themselves that they are indeed on the straight path, and that they indeed have a true understanding of God and what he expects from us. To simply rely on the scholarly work of others is to trust your eternity to their judgment, their interpretation, and in some cases, even their opinion.

This doesn't mean, however, that we must completely abandon the scholarly work of others; on the contrary, we should take advantage of every resource available and evaluate it according to our own judgment. If we are sincere in our search for the truth, God will surely guide us to it.

Some would say it is wrong to question your religion, and that certain things should just be accepted on faith, but is it wrong for someone to seek a better understanding of his/her religion? All religions are based to a certain extent on faith, but faith should not require us to accept ideologies that stand contrary to reason. Belief in a God that can't be seen, for example, requires faith, but it does not conflict in any way with logic or reason. The signs of God's existence are all around us; everyone can see them, but only those with faith can understand them.

Both Islam and Christianity require faith in matters of the "unseen," although Islam, unlike Christianity, does not require faith in mysterious doctrines like the Trinity, which presents a mathematical quagmire of epic proportions wherein one God exists in three persons. Nevertheless, we cannot say that every belief pertaining to Christianity is based on faulty reasoning because many of the beliefs held in Christianity are also found in Islam, such as the miraculous birth of Jesus and the fact that he performed miracles as an adult. These events may be difficult to believe, but they do not require some elaborate explanation that can never be fully understood, like the Trinity.

It is often argued that all religions are basically the same, instilling good moral conduct and wholesome values, and that no one should, therefore, be encouraged to follow one religion over another. Those who usually subscribe to this line of thinking, however, are either totally agnostic or less than devout members of some organized religion. Indeed, none of the mainstream world religions could promote such a concept because to do so would render that religion irrelevant. Surely we cannot imagine that Abraham, Moses, or Jesus would have offered people the option to either accept the message they delivered or continue in their old ways.

This is not to say that there should be no such thing as religious tolerance. Neither Jesus nor Muhammad forced their religion on anyone. The point is that no prophet has ever embraced the notion that all religions (or gods) are equal, or that salvation is achievable through the religion of your choice. It stands to reason, then, that there can only be one ultimate truth regarding the divine and the unseen (heaven, hell, life after death), and when you think about it, if a religion does not instill in the hearts and minds of its adherents the desire to invite others with confidence in the validity of their faith, there is obviously something lacking in either the religion itself or the person attempting to follow it.

Islam, like Christianity, is a universal religion with an open invitation to people of all nations. The Koran, however, is unique in the way that it addresses people of other faiths. There are verses in the Koran addressed to the entire human race, verses that are addressed specifically to believers, and verses that are directed to the "People of the Book," meaning Jews and Christians. The Jews are additionally addressed in the Koran as the Children of Israel, while Christians are referred to as the Nazoreans.

Among the many verses in the Koran that are addressed to Christians is the following invitation to accept the message of pure monotheism delivered by Prophet Muhammad:

> Say: "O People of the Book! Come to common terms as between us and you: That we worship none but Allah (God); that we associate no partners with him; that we erect not, from among ourselves, Lords and patrons other than Allah (God)." (Al-Imran:64)

The importance of monotheism and the unity of God is an underlying theme stressed throughout the Bible and, according to Jesus (as related by Mark), the most important of all commandments.[1] According to mainstream Christianity, the unity of God is upheld in the Trinity, however, the usage of this term is denounced in the Koran:

> O people of the Book! Do not exceed the limits in your religion, nor say of Allah aught but the truth. The Messiah, son of Mary, was (no more than) a messenger of Allah and his

---

[1]   See Mark 12:28–29.

word, which he bestowed on Mary and a spirit from him. So believe in Allah and his messengers. Say not: "Three (trinity)!" Cease! (It is) better for you. Indeed Allah is One God. Far exalted is he above having a son. (An-Nisa'a:171)

Thus, are the Christians encouraged to abandon the Trinity and return to the religion of true monotheism prescribed in the Bible and confirmed in the Koran. In addition to this, they are directed to believe in all of the messengers of Allah (i.e., the prophets), including Muhammad, the final messenger of Allah (God). The message of Muhammad (i.e., the Koran) encompasses all that was revealed before it, including the Torah and the Gospel, and has been protected from corruption in a way that no other revelation before it has.

The authenticity of the Koran is well documented and practically irrefutable. For one thing, it has remained extant in the language (Arabic) it was revealed and is only recited in this language. Translations are used for educational purposes, but all interpretations refer back to the original Arabic text. The Koran is recited consistently in a precise manner based on clearly defined rules, which are routinely enforced through instruction and mutual oversight. Countless Muslims have memorized the Koran in its entirety since the time of Muhammad, making it virtually indestructible, many of whom belong to a chain of instructors that can be traced back to the Prophet himself.

Although the primary means of preserving the Koran is through memorization, it is also widely reported that the

Koran was written down during the lifetime of the Prophet and compiled into one volume shortly after his death. Today there are still written copies of the Koran in existence that date back to the time of Uthman ibn Affan, a close companion of Muhammad, which are virtually identical to any modern copy of the Koran.

The author of the Koran identifies himself in several verses as Allah,[1] the Arabic word for God. The words of the Koran were revealed to the Prophet piecemeal[2] over a period of twenty-three years through the angel Gabriel—presumably the same angel that appears to Mary and Zechariah in the Gospel according to Luke.[3] When Muhammad began reciting the Koran to his people, many of them called him a liar, and some thought he had gone mad. To others, the words of the Koran had a profound effect and changed their lives forever.[4]

Today the Koran is generally regarded as a fabrication among the critics of Islam. It is also believed that Muhammad borrowed material from the Bible to create the Koran. Those who dismiss the Koran, however, do so not because of any

---

[1]   See chapter 10, verse 37 of the Holy Koran.

[2]   See chapter 17, verse 106 of the Holy Koran.

[3]   See Luke 1:5–38 in the sacred Bible.

[4]   Omar ibn al-Khattab, who eventually became the second caliph, was on his way to kill Muhammad when he learned of his sister's conversion to Islam and, after striking her in a fit of rage, decided to read a sample from the Koran himself. When the soon-to-be great leader read from what he recognized to be the words of Allah, he became so moved that he immediately ran to the Prophet and embraced Islam.

deficiency or discrepancy within the book itself, but rather, they reject Islam because they have no use for it. The Jews, for example, have been waiting for a Messiah to arise from the lineage of David and restore the kingdom of Israel, and since Muhammad was an Arab, who rebuked them for rejecting the Messiah, they cannot accept him as a legitimate prophet. Christians, meanwhile, believe that Jesus came in fulfillment of the law (*Torah*) and the prophets of the Hebrew Scripture and, thus, have no room for Muhammad or the Koran either. If one were to examine the Koran, however, with an open mind and without any preconceived notions, he/she would, at the very least, be forced to admit that the Koran is an amazing book that cannot be easily explained away as a product of human intellect. The fact that the Koran consistently describes natural phenomenon in full agreement with modern science,[1] despite the fact that it was revealed more than fourteen centuries ago, or that nowhere in its six hundred plus pages does the Koran contradict itself, should certainly cause the man of reason to ponder the possibility that this book is from none other than Allah (God). When we add to this the fact that Muhammad was illiterate, the task of explaining the Koran becomes increasingly difficult.

According to most contemporary biblical scholars the Torah was compiled from multiple sources long after the time of Moses, although many still cling to the traditional view that Moses himself authored this crucial segment of the Hebrew Bible. The earliest manuscripts (or scrolls) available today in the Hebrew language belong to the tenth century

---

[1]   See Appendix A.

CE—more than two thousand years after the time of Moses, which makes it difficult to believe that the original text has survived. The Codex Vaticanus, which dates from the fourth century CE, contains an older Greek translation of the Hebrew Bible but is still several centuries removed from the original composition. The Codex Vaticanus is also believed to contain some of the oldest and most reliable manuscripts of the New Testament. The exact origin of this important document, however, is unknown.

The gospels we have today were written initially, or so it seems, by four different evangelists and then subsequently copied (and translated) to the point where none of the original manuscripts have survived. Upon reading these texts one notes that each evangelist presents a unique account of Jesus's ministry from a narrator's point of view, while including his own words along with statements allegedly uttered by Jesus and others. According to popular tradition these books were authored by individuals connected to the apostolic age, although many doubts have arisen in recent years, particularly in regard to the authorship of the first Gospel (Matthew) and portions of the fourth Gospel (John).

The fact that the first Gospel is based to a large extent on the Gospel according to Mark, which predates it, makes it difficult to accept as the work of Matthew the disciple because Matthew, as a member of "the Twelve" (disciples commissioned by Jesus), should have had no reason to rely upon someone else as a source in lieu of his own testimony. The author of the second Gospel—believed to be John Mark, a cousin of Barnabas—was not one of the Twelve and had to rely himself upon the testimony of others. It should also be noted that during the first and second centuries of the Christian era pseudonymous writings were common.

In regard to the fourth Gospel, modern researchers believe that the original work has been edited and to it were added the prologue and one additional chapter.

The authorship of the third Gospel (Luke) is seldom contested, although the author himself admits in the opening of his first book that he was not an eyewitness to the events recorded in his two-volume work.[1]

The Koran acknowledges the divine origin of both the Torah and the Gospel[2]; however, those to whom this revelation has been entrusted (i.e., the Jews and the Christians) are encouraged in the Koran to embrace the new revelation that was given to Muhammad in addition to the scriptures they already have/had.[3] In other words, the Koran does not necessarily reject these previous scriptures, but rather, *confirms*[4] them. In fact, the Koran even demands that those who believe in Muhammad and his message must also believe in the scriptures that were sent down before him.[5]

---

[1]   Luke is believed to be not only the author of the third Gospel but also the author of Acts of the Apostles.

[2]   See chapter 3, verses 2–3 of the Holy Koran.

[3]   See chapter 4, verse 47 of the Holy Koran.

[4]   The word that appears in the Arabic text, *musaddiq*, comes from the root word *sadaqa*, which means, "to speak the truth." Hence, the Koran speaks the truth about the Bible.

[5]   See chapter 4, verse 136 of the Holy Koran.

The Bible, therefore, from an Islamic perspective, must contain some remnant of truth, and the criterion for determining truth from falsehood should be the Koran itself.

Prophet Muhammad did not claim to be the founder of an entirely new religion but rather called people to the way of the prophets that preceded him. The Koran is filled with lessons from these prophets, of which many parallels can be found in the Bible as well. It should, therefore, come as no surprise to learn that in many ways the Bible is more in line with the teaching of Islam than the doctrines set forth by the church, particularly with regard to Jesus and his relationship with God.

The authors of the New Testament admired Jesus more than any other man, including Moses, but at no time did they ever confuse him with God. Expressions like "Son of God" and "Lord Jesus"—as we shall see during the course of this discussion—did not hold for them the same meaning that the clerics of later generations derived from them. These intriguing appellations were intended to promote Jesus as the Messiah, Son of David, in accordance with the scriptures, and nothing more. Thus, Jesus was distinguished, not only from the rest of humanity, but also from the one who created him and anointed him. Throughout the Christian canon Jesus is depicted as a true man and a servant of God, just as he is in the Koran and, although at times the line between the Creator and the created may seem a bit obscure, the authors of these sacred manuscripts never fail to differentiate between the Almighty and his anointed.

Although most of the verses that deal with Jesus in the Bible are consistent with the Islamic view of Christ, many are interpreted in ways that support doctrines rejected by Islam. In the following document we shall examine those verses objectively that seem to support the mainstream Christian belief that Jesus is God; the intent being to explore all plausible interpretations, including the traditional interpretation of the verse, and let the reader determine for him/herself exactly what the Bible says about Jesus.

In evaluating these scriptures we will refer when necessary to the Greek and Hebrew versions of the Bible in an effort to obtain the best possible and most accurate interpretation of the text. At the same time we will examine each verse with the context of the passage in mind and investigate other verses that relate in whatever way to the verse in question. Most importantly, we will apply the litmus test of reason at all times during the course of this discussion.

In some cases it will be necessary to consider the authenticity of a passage, as it is not realistic to imagine that each and every verse in the entire Christian canon could be reconciled with the Islamic view of Christ. For the most part, however, we will assume authenticity from the estimated time of composition, which for some portions of the Bible is more than one hundred years after the ascension of Jesus.

CHAPTER 1

Son of God

"Son of God" is one of the most common titles applied to Jesus in the Bible and for centuries has been perhaps the most popular nomenclature used among Christian clergy to describe Jesus. The exact meaning of this expression, however, is anything but clear, and, in fact, any attempt to explain it is bound to yield more questions than answers.

According to mainstream Christianity Jesus, as the Son of God, is of the same *essence* as God and, thus, shares in his divinity, along with the Holy Spirit, and the three (Father, Son, and Holy Spirit) combine to form one triune deity. This belief, however, was adopted only after years of intense debate and did not become officially part of the Christian creed until the fourth century of the church, when the leaders of various Christian communities began holding what became a series of ecumenical councils aimed at resolving disputes and stamping out heresy.

The Trinity itself is a later development found nowhere in Christian literature prior to the end of the second century CE. The fact that the word *trinity* does not appear anywhere in the Bible indicates that the early evangelists—those who claimed to deliver the message of Jesus and whose writings were later canonized by the church—knew nothing of the

Trinity and, thus, could not have understood the expression "Son of God" in terms of the Trinity.

In both the Hebrew Bible and the Christian canon the word "Father" is used in reference to God in his entirety without any implication that he—either God or the Father—coexists with other entities. In the book of Deuteronomy, for instance, when Moses is near his death, he admonishes his nation: "Do ye thus requite the LORD, O foolish people and unwise? *is not he thy father* that hath bought thee? hath he not made thee, and established thee?" (Deut. 32:6, KJV). Similarly, in the Gospel according to John, when a group of believing Jews proclaims: "we have one Father, even God," Jesus replies: "If God were your Father, ye would love me" (John 8:41–42, KJV).

The Jews supposedly object, however, when Jesus reportedly says: "My Father worketh hitherto, and I work" (John 5:17, KJV) after being criticized for healing on the Sabbath. According to the author or narrator of the gospel, when the Jews hear Jesus refer to God as "my Father" they try to kill him because "he not only had broken the sabbath, but said also that God was his Father, making himself equal with God" (John 5:18, KJV).

Jesus, of course, did not intend to make himself "equal with God" and thus goes on to explain that, although he was reportedly able to heal the sick and raise the dead, it was the Father who *showed* him these works and that "of himself" the Son could do nothing (John 5:19–21, KJV).

"I can of mine own self do nothing," says Jesus, later in the passage, "as I hear, I judge: and my judgment is just; because I seek not mine own will, but the will of the Father which hath sent me" (John 5:30, KJV).

According to a number of Christian commentaries, when Jesus refers to God as "my Father" in the Bible he is alluding to his divine relationship with the Father in regard to the Trinity, and this, they submit, should not be confused with expressions like "our Father", "your Father," or "the Father," as these apply to the relationship between God and ordinary believers.

As a prophet of God and his anointed servant, Jesus undoubtedly enjoyed a close relationship with the "Father," but to say that he is equal to God just because he called him *my Father* is an unfounded postulation that defies all logic and reason. If the disciples of Jesus could refer to God as "our Father," as they were instructed in the Gospel according to Matthew (Matt. 6:9), then certainly Jesus should be able to call him "my Father" without being accused of blasphemy. After all, in the Gospel according to John, Jesus not only refers to the Almighty as "my Father," but also describes him as "my God":

> Jesus saith unto her, Touch me not; for I am not yet ascended to my Father: but go to my brethren, and say unto them, I ascend unto my Father, and your Father; and *to my God, and your God.* (John 20:17, KJV)

In his first letter to the Corinthians, Paul writes: "But to us there is but one God, the Father, of whom are all things" (1

Cor. 8:6, KJV), indicating clearly his belief in the unity of God. Paul did not say we have one God, the Father, Son, and Holy Spirit. The "Father" alone is God, he says.

Yes, it is true that Paul goes on to say in the same verse that, in addition to the one God, the believers had also "one Lord, Jesus Christ, *through* whom are all things" (1 Cor. 8:6, ASV), but this in no way implies that Jesus is part of the one God. The fact that Paul makes such a clear distinction between God, the Father, and Jesus, the Lord, essentially proves that he did not believe in the triune godhead that later evolved into church dogma.

In their extreme admiration and love for Jesus, the early evangelists at times portrayed their master in ways that could easily be misinterpreted, but never did they confuse him with God. Regardless of how much praise is attributed to Jesus in the New Testament, some distinction, however subtle, is always made between God and Jesus.

As the Messiah, Jesus was thought of as the link *through* which the believers could access the "Father" and, conversely, the one *through* whom God would act, as he did when Jesus performed his miraculous healings. In his second book, Acts of the Apostles, Luke[1] explains how God would judge the world *through* Jesus:

> And the times of this ignorance God winked
> at; but now commandeth all men every

---

[1]   Acts of the Apostles opens with a reference to an earlier book, most likely Luke's gospel, because both Acts and the Gospel according to Luke are addressed to a ruler named Theophilus.

> where to repent: Because he hath appointed
> a day, in the which *he will judge the world*
> *in righteousness by*[1] *that man whom he hath*
> *ordained*; whereof he hath given assurance
> unto all men, in that he hath raised him from
> the dead. (Acts 17:30–31, KJV)

Thus, when we read Paul's statement that there is one God "of whom are all things" and one Lord "*through* whom are all things" (1 Cor. 8:6, ASV), we can understand this as another way of expressing the same subordinate relationship between God and Jesus, wherein God is viewed as the source of "all things" and Jesus, the medium through which God attends to "all things," or to all matters. Christian scholars unfortunately interpret these words as an indication that Jesus took part in Creation and is, therefore, equal to God, but in doing so they ignore the clear distinction Paul makes in the verse between God, the Father, and Jesus, the Lord, as well as the expression of subordination he makes later in the epistle between God and Jesus:

> Now I praise you, brethren, that ye remember
> me in all things, and keep the ordinances, as I
> delivered them to you. But I would have you
> know, that the head of every man is Christ;
> and the head of the woman is the man; and
> *the head of Christ is God*. (1 Cor. 11:2–3, KJV)

To illustrate further the conviction of Paul's Unitarian beliefs, let us consider the proclamation of faith he imparts

---

[1]   The Greek preposition, "en" is often translated as "by" but could also mean *through*. In the New American (Catholic) Bible, the word "en" is translated as *through* in Acts 17:31.

on Timothy, wherein the Messiah is unequivocally defined as a man in contrast to God:

> For there is one God, and one mediator between God and men, *the man* Christ Jesus. (1 Tim. 2:5, KJV)

And if that's not enough, we can refer to Paul's letter to the Ephesians where the so-called apostle declares: "Blessed be *the God* and Father *of our Lord* Jesus Christ" (Eph. 1:3, KJV).

The Greek word for son, *huios*, was used extensively by the early evangelists, both in the literal sense—in reference to male offspring—and, perhaps more abundantly, in the allegorical sense to define various individuals and groups of people in terms of character or behavior. In the Gospel according to John, for example, Jesus refers to Judas, the disciple who allegedly betrayed him, as the "son of perdition" (John 17:12, KJV) in order to identify him as someone associated with evil or destruction, while in the Gospel according to Matthew the "sons of the kingdom" (i.e., the followers of Christ) are contrasted with the "sons of the evil one," those led astray by the devil (Matt. 13:38, ASV).[1]

In his letter to the Romans, Paul states that, although Jesus had been "born of the seed of David according to the flesh," he was "declared to be the Son of God… by the resurrection from the dead" (Rom. 1:3–4, ASV), which means that, in Paul's view, Jesus was biologically a descendent of David and

---

[1]   In many translations of the Bible the English term *children* appears in lieu of *sons* when the source word *huios* is applied to a group of people.

did not become truly "Son of God" until after he was raised from the dead, or, in other words, Paul did not believe that Jesus was literally the Son of God; he merely thought of him as "Son of God" in the allegorical sense.

Elsewhere in the book of Romans, when Paul refers to the followers of Christ as "sons of God" (Rom. 8:14, KJV), the significance of this appellation, so ardently proclaimed of Jesus, erodes even further, as the Messiah is joined by others in this distinction, and when Jesus himself applies the term to those who make peace (Matt. 5:9) in the Gospel according to Matthew, or to those who "shall be accounted worthy to obtain that world, and the resurrection from the dead" (Luke 20:35–36, KJV) in the Gospel according to Luke, it becomes eminently clear that "Son of God" is not a title that denotes divinity, but rather, an expression that conveys a quality of righteousness, piety, and closeness with God.

In contrast, we find, in the Gospel according to John, Jesus telling the disbelieving Jews: "Ye are of your father the devil, and the lusts of your father ye will do" (John 8:44, KJV). Although the Jews were physically descendants of Abraham, their disobedience and rejection of Jesus made them *children of the devil* in a figurative sense. Similarly, when Jesus and his followers are designated as "sons of God" in the Bible, it should be understood as figurative speech symbolizing their relationship with God, and not taken literally.

The author of the fourth Gospel uses the Greek term *monogenes* in conjunction with *huios*, making Jesus the "only begotten Son" of God, or in modern versions, God's "only Son":

> For God so loved the world, that he gave his
> *only begotten* (monogenes) *Son* (huios), that
> whosoever believeth in him should not perish,
> but have everlasting life. (John 3:16, KJV)

From the context of the passage, it's difficult to discern exactly what "John" meant by the use of this term. The word *monogenes* is used only in eight other New Testament verses, and John is the only one who uses the term in relation to Jesus. The term primarily denotes exclusiveness in regard to children. It can be used together with "son" (*huios*) or by itself, with the gender of the child implied. It is conceivable that John employed the term *monogenes* as a subtle way of affirming his belief in the virgin birth of Jesus, although the fact that the evangelist makes no mention of this miraculous event in any of the five books attributed to him would seem to suggest he had no knowledge of it. Moreover, in the beginning of the fourth Gospel, as Jesus is rounding up his disciples, John relates a dialog between Philip and Nathanael, wherein Philip refers to Jesus as "the son of Joseph" (John 1:45, KJV), as if Joseph was his natural father.

Perhaps the most likely explanation for John's use of the term *monogenes* is that the evangelist sought to form an exclusive title for Jesus. In the gospel attributed to John, the words "Son of God" are reserved for Jesus, and only once[1] in the five books that bear the name John is anyone other than Jesus referred to as a son of God. Furthermore, it is quite

---

[1]   See Rev. 21:7.

possible that the author of this one verse that stands out as an exception is not the same author who wrote, "For God so loved the world that he gave his only begotten (*monogenes*) Son." (John 3:16, above).

In the Gospel according to Matthew, after witnessing the miracle of Jesus walking on water, the disciples proclaim to their master: "Of a truth thou art the Son of God" (Matt. 14:33, KJV), thereby implying that the impetus for applying this honorable designation to Jesus was based, not on the circumstances surrounding his birth, but rather, the prophethood of Jesus, which was confirmed through the performance of these miracles. In the Gospel according to John, the prophet himself explains: "the works which the Father hath given me to finish… bear witness of me, that the Father hath sent me" (John 5:36, KJV), meaning that the purpose behind these miracles, or "works," was to demonstrate Jesus's standing with God and to stifle critics.

Elsewhere in the Gospel according to Matthew, after Jesus heals a paralytic, the narrator stresses that those who witnessed this miracle "marvelled, and glorified God, which had given such power unto men" (Matt. 9:8, KJV). They did not glorify Jesus because, as Jews, they knew that God was the one who allowed these miracles to occur, and that he had given authority to Jesus, a mere human, just as he had given authority to Moses and others before him.

Although John is the only author in the entire Christian canon who identifies Jesus as God's "only Son" Jesus is frequently designated as THE Son of God in other parts of the Bible, which alludes to a distinction that was undoubtedly associated with this title when applied to Jesus, and so, in the interest of determining exactly what the early evangelists meant when they referred to Christ as "the Son of God," let us begin by examining the only passage in the Bible in which the prophet refers to himself as Son of God.

In the Gospel according to John, when asked by a group of Jews in the temple: "If thou be the Christ, tell us plainly," Jesus answers in the affirmative, albeit indirectly, saying: "I told you, and ye believed not," and then goes on to explain the relationship between he and his followers in contrast to the disbelief of the Jews with whom he was speaking (John 10:24–27, KJV). It is not until he proclaims: "I and the Father are one" (John 10:30–31), however, that the crowd takes offense and begins to throw stones at Jesus, and when the prophet asks why they are stoning him, the Jews say: "because that thou, being a man, makest thyself God" (John 10:33, KJV).

In response to this harsh accusation Jesus recites a verse from scripture and then proceeds to explain the meaning behind his previous statement:

> "*Is it not written in your law, I said, Ye are gods*? If he called them gods, unto whom the word of God came, and the scripture cannot be broken; Say ye of him, whom the Father hath sanctified, and sent into the world, Thou blasphemest; because I said, I am the Son of God?" (John 10:34–36, KJV)

Christian clerics generally interpret this as a claim of divinity made by Jesus based on the indirect reference he makes to himself as Son of God. It's important to note, however, that the prophet uses this title in defense against a claim of blasphemy, pointing out to the Jews that in their own scripture ordinary, mortal men were metaphorically referred to as both gods and sons of God:

> I have said, Ye are gods; and all of you are children of the most High. But ye shall die like men. (Ps. 82:6–7, KJV)

Rather than confirming their suspicions, Jesus reasoned with the Jews that, as the Messiah—the one "whom the Father hath sanctified, and sent into the world"—he could not be guilty of blasphemy for claiming to be "one" with the Father, or "Son of God," if others before him enjoyed similar, if not greater status in the scriptures.[1] Jesus demonstrated clearly through his knowledge of the law and works (miracles) of faith that he was worthy of any title or attribute assigned to anyone in the scriptures, other than God.

The Jews at the time of Jesus presumably made no distinction between the Messiah and the Son of God, as in the Gospel according to Mark; when Jesus appears before the Sanhedrin, he is reportedly asked by the presiding high priest: "Art thou the Christ,[2] the Son of the Blessed?" (Mark 14:61, KJV), while in the Gospel according to Matthew, in a parallel account of the same event, the high priest exclaims:

---

[1]   The passage that Jesus quotes (Ps. 82) is believed to be in reference to the leaders of Israel who were appointed as judges at the time of Moses (see Deut. 1:15–17).

[2]   The English words Christ and Messiah are both derived from the Hebrew word *Mashiach*.

"I adjure thee by the living God, that thou tell us whether thou be the Christ, the Son of God" (Matt. 26:63, KJV).[1] The Jews did, however, make a distinction between God and the Messiah, evidently, or else they would not have accused Jesus of blasphemy after asking him sincerely if he was the Messiah. It can be said, therefore, as the evidence would seem to suggest, that in the language of the early Judeo-Christian community the Son of God was nothing more than a prophet or leader, not to be confused with God, and more specifically, the long-awaited prophet known as the Messiah, and so the question then becomes: who, or what, is the Messiah?

The word Messiah comes from the Hebrew word *Mashiach,* which means, "anointed." In the Hebrew scripture, the word *Mashiach* is used in reference to priests and kings who were *anointed* by God as a form of consecration or validation of their positions. In the Pentateuch, for example, Moses is instructed by God to anoint Aaron and his sons as priests for generations to come (Exod. 40:12–15), while in the historic books Saul (1 Sam. 10:1), David (2 Sam. 5:3), and Solomon (1 Kings 1:39) are anointed as kings of Israel. The Greek word for anointed, *Christos*, was developed into the epithet *Christ* and applied exclusively to Jesus sometime after his departure from the world.

In Jewish tradition the "King Messiah" or "Messiah, son of David" refers to a specific messiah that would, among other things, initiate the messianic age. The messianic age is described in a variety of ways in the prophetic writings

---

[1]   See also Matt. 16:16, John 11:27, and John 20:31.

of the Old Testament, but one recurring theme is that the Children of Israel are to have at this time temporal power over "the nations." Numerous prophecies pertaining to the Messiah and the messianic age can be found in the Hebrew scriptures, although opinions vary among scholars as to the exact meaning of these often-obscure passages.

The early evangelists presumably believed that Jesus came in fulfillment of these prophecies, as they went to great lengths to convince others that Jesus was indeed the Messiah, son of David, whom the Jews had been waiting for. In fact, proving that Jesus was the Messiah is the primary objective of virtually every book in the Christian canon.

The connection between the *Messiah* and the *Son of God* can be traced back to the second book of Samuel, where the God of Israel, speaking through Nathan,[1] tells David: "When thy days are fulfilled, and thou shalt sleep with thy fathers, I will set up thy seed after thee, that shall proceed out of thy bowels, and I will establish his kingdom. He shall build a house for my name, and I will establish the throne of his kingdom for ever. *I will be his father, and he shall be my son*" (2 Sam. 7:12–14, ASV). Jews and Christians alike interpret this as a promise to the Children of Israel of permanent and universal restoration of God's rule through the Messiah; the difference being that, while the Jews expect immediate results from the Messiah, Christians believe that, although the restoration, or "kingdom of God," began with the resurrection of Jesus, it will not be fully realized until

---

[1]   In the Old Testament, Nathan is a prophet closely associated with King David.

he returns "in his glory." Regardless of how or when this restoration would take place, however, it is obvious from the context of the passage that the Messiah would not be equal to God because immediately after declaring that the anointed heir of David "shall be my son," the God of Israel continues: "If he commit iniquity, I will chasten him with the rod of men, and with the stripes of the children of men" (2 Sam. 7:14, KJV).

For the Jews at the time of Jesus, it was incumbent on the Messiah to restore the kingdom of David, as evidenced in the gospel narratives when Jesus makes his triumphant entry into Jerusalem, and the crowd of people waiting for him there shouts, "Blessed be the kingdom of our father David, that cometh" (Mark 11:10, KJV) in anticipation of him performing this task. The hopes of these people (if the report is true) were undoubtedly shattered when they witnessed what appeared to be the Crucifixion of their Messiah.

After the Crucifixion, when the disciples reportedly ask: "Lord, wilt thou at this time restore again the kingdom to Israel?" Jesus explains: "It is not for you to know the times or the seasons, which the Father hath put in his own power" (Acts 1:6–7, KJV). The power, or authority, to restore the kingdom, in other words, did not belong to Jesus. Ultimately it would be God, the "Father," who would restore the kingdom of Israel. The role of the Messiah in the restoration of Israel would be like the role of Moses in the Exodus from Egypt, as Peter alludes to during his speech in the temple area, where immediately after addressing the issue of restoration he draws a comparison between Moses and Jesus:

> Repent ye therefore, and be converted, that
> your sins may be blotted out, when the times
> of refreshing shall come from the presence
> of the Lord. And he shall send Jesus Christ,
> which before was preached unto you: Whom
> the heaven must receive until the times of
> restitution of all things, which God hath
> spoken by the mouth of all his holy prophets
> since the world began. *For Moses truly said*
> *unto the fathers, A prophet shall the Lord*
> *your God raise up unto you of your brethren,*
> *like unto me; him shall ye hear in all things*
> *whatsoever he shall say unto you.* (Acts 3:19–
> 22, KJV)

Elsewhere in the New Testament, Jesus is compared to Moses by the author of Hebrews, and both are described as faithful to God:

> Wherefore, holy brethren, partakers of the
> heavenly calling, consider the Apostle and
> High Priest of our profession, *Christ Jesus;*
> *Who was faithful to him that appointed him,*
> *as also Moses was faithful in all his house.*
> (Heb. 3:1–2, KJV)

As the Messiah, Jesus was expected to "reign over the house of Jacob for ever" (Luke 1:33, KJV). It was understood, however, that this reign would not begin until after the *Parousia* ("coming" of Christ), or as Peter explains, "until the times of restitution of all things" (Acts 3:21, above). In Jewish tradition this is known as the messianic age—a time when, according to the prophet Isaiah, there would be no more death (Isa. 25:8). In the book of Revelation Jesus reigns at some point for a "thousand years" along with those who were martyred for their testimony of Christ (Rev. 20:4), but the permanent restoration of Jerusalem does not occur until after God descends on his throne to judge all who had been dead and to dwell with mankind (Rev. 20:11–21:3).

The Koran, like the Bible, refers to Jesus as the Messiah but, unlike the Bible, rebukes those who call him Son of God. In the fifth *Surah*, or chapter, of the Koran, Allah (God) says: "Verily, they have disbelieved who say, 'Allah is the Messiah, son of Mary'" (Al-Maidah:72), while in another verse it is stated, in so many words, that Allah is far exalted above having a son (An-Nisa':171). To the authors of the New Testament, "Son of God" was evidently an expression used to emphasize their belief that Jesus was the Messiah, but by the time the Koran was revealed the expression had become synonymous with God, due to the evolution of the Trinitarian doctrine. Therefore, it could no longer be acceptable to refer to Jesus in this manner.

This is not to say that the use of this terminology had been sanctioned by Jesus or his disciples. None of the twenty-seven books that make up the New Testament can be connected conclusively to them. The point is that those who did contribute to the Christian canon demonstrated consistently, for the most part, that they believed in the unity of God, and so the Son of God to them was just another name for the Messiah.

The miraculous nature in which Jesus was conceived is compared in the Koran to the creation of Adam:

> Verily, the likeness of Jesus before Allah is the
> likeness of Adam. He created him from dust,
> then said to him: "Be!"—then (immediately)
> he came into being. (Al-'Imran:59)

Having been created without father or mother, Adam, if anyone, deserves to be called "Son of God" more than Jesus, although both men, according to the Koran, were created through the word, or commandment, of Allah.

The genealogy of Jesus, as recorded by Matthew and Luke, reveals that, on the issue of ancestry and origin, the early evangelists regarded Jesus not as the Son of God, but rather a son of David.

According to Luke, Jesus was thought to be a son of Joseph, and Adam is referred to as the Son of God:

> And Jesus himself began to be about thirty
> years of age, being (as was supposed) *the son
> of Joseph.* (Luke 3:23, KJV)

> Which was the son of Enos, which was the
> son of Seth, which was the son of *Adam,
> which was the son of God.* (Luke 3:38, KJV)

Joseph is reported as a descendent of David by Mathew, as well as Luke, and both evangelists trace the genealogy of Jesus through Joseph, who, according to Matthew (Matt. 1:24–25), took Mary into his home prior to the birth of Jesus.

Luke also mentions in his gospel that Jesus "shall be *called* the Son of the Highest" (Luke 1:32, KJV), but this in no way implies that he is divine, or even unique, because the same thing was allegedly said about people who make peace in the Gospel according to Matthew:

> Blessed are the peacemakers: for they shall
> be called sons of God. (Matt. 5:9, ASV)

In the Koran, Jesus is called "Son of Mary," in what would seem to be a subtle way of confirming the miraculous nature of his birth, while at the same time, denouncing any notion that he is God. In ancient Hebrew culture (as well as Arab culture), it was customary to refer to a person as the son or daughter of his or her father, or some other paternal ancestor, but since Jesus had no father, he could not rightfully be named in this manner, and so by calling the Messiah Son of Mary the Koran accentuates the fact that Jesus had no paternal ancestry whatsoever.

Interestingly enough, Mark is the only evangelist who identifies Jesus as the son of Mary, and even he employs the expression only once, while relating a scene in Nazareth where the prophet returns to his hometown to teach (Mark 6:1–3). In the Gospel according to Matthew, during a parallel account of the same incident, the people of Nazareth refer to Jesus as "the carpenter's son" (Matt. 13:55, KJV), indicating that they considered him to be the son of Joseph, while in Luke's version of the event the people ask: "Is not this Joseph's son" (Luke 4:22, KJV)?

For the authors of the New Testament it was probably more important to promote Jesus as the son of David—in the interest of making him the Messiah—than to try to prove that he was born miraculously, and certainly less difficult. Even in the infancy narratives, the only two passages in the entire Christian canon that even mention the miraculous birth of Jesus, the son of Mary is conspicuously identified as a descendent of David:

> The book of the generation of Jesus Christ, *the son of David*, the son of Abraham. (Matt. 1:1, KJV)

> He shall be great, and shall be called the Son of the Highest: and the Lord God shall give unto him the throne of *his father David*. (Luke 1:32, KJV)

The reason for this blatant contradiction is anyone's guess. Perhaps the authors of these sacred texts believed that Joseph's seed was miraculously placed in the womb of Mary while she remained a virgin, or maybe they simply regarded Jesus as a son of David through adoption into the "house" of David.

It is also worth noting that Mark, the only author in the entire Christian canon to identify Jesus as the son of Mary, is also the only gospel narrator who does not explicitly state that Jesus was a descendent of David, although he does report others referring to the Messiah as "Son of David."[1] In contrast to this we have Paul, who describes Jesus not only as the *Son* of David, but even the "seed" of David:

> Paul, a servant of Jesus Christ, called to be an apostle, separated unto the gospel of

---

[1]   Mark 10:47–48.

> God, (Which he had promised afore by his
> prophets in the holy scriptures,) Concerning
> his Son Jesus Christ our Lord, which was
> made of *the seed of David* according to the
> flesh. (Rom. 1:1–3, KJV)

The word "seed" that appears in the translation of this verse is derived from the Greek word *sperma*, which also corresponds to the English word *sperm* and is often used in the New Testament—as it is here—in reference to the biological descendents of Abraham. Paul apparently assumed, like most of the people of the time, that Jesus was Joseph's biological son. As a latecomer to the Christian community, Paul could not have had the same knowledge as the disciples who heard him preach both publicly and privately, and, consequently, Paul does not quote Jesus anywhere in his epistles. The authors of the synoptic Gospels, on the other hand, sought to preserve the oral tradition of Jesus, which incidentally contains nothing to confirm any such biological connection to David. In fact, Jesus, in the synoptic Gospels, essentially denies the notion that he is a descendent of David:

> And Jesus answered and said, while he taught
> in the temple, How say the scribes that Christ
> is the son of David? For David himself said
> by the Holy Ghost, The LORD said to my
> Lord, Sit thou on my right hand, till I make
> thine enemies thy footstool. David therefore
> himself calleth him Lord; and whence is he
> then his son?[1] (Mark 12:35–37, KJV)

---

[1]   See also Matt. 22:41–46 and Luke 20:41–44.

Despite the fact that these early evangelists knew about the miraculous conception of Jesus "of the Holy Spirit" (Matt. 1:18), they did not jump to the conclusion that God was literally the father of Jesus. In fact, Matthew refers to Jesus as "Son of God" for the first time during the temptation in the wilderness scene, when Jesus was a full-grown adult (Matt. 4:3). Mark refers to Jesus only once himself as Son of God—in the opening verse of his gospel—however, not all of the ancient manuscripts contain the words "Son of God" in this verse. Luke says only that Jesus would be "called" Son of God during his infancy narrative (Luke 1:35) and then, like Matthew, waits until the temptation scene to use the term again.

In one verse Luke effectively summarizes the very premise of this discussion, viz. that Jesus was only called the Son of God; he was not literally a descendent of the Almighty Creator. Unfortunately, this title, through centuries of conflict and excessive admiration of Jesus, has been transformed into a blasphemous term unbeknownst to the modern-day followers of Christ. The fact of the matter is that Jesus was neither the Son of God nor the son of David; he was the son of Mary and, as the evidence shows, these titles were applied to him by the early evangelists, not for the purpose of deification, but rather, to promote their master as the long-awaited Messiah and king of Israel.

CHAPTER 2

Lord

The deification of Christ by the founders of orthodox Christianity is undoubtedly attributable, at least in part, to the fact that both Jesus and the God of Israel are referred to in the Bible as Lord. Although the oneness of God is repeatedly contrasted in these texts against the unwavering obedience and servitude of Jesus, the ambiguity of the term, together with the wording of certain passages, makes it difficult at times to differentiate between the Lord God and the Lord Jesus, and this, unfortunately, has left open the door to innovation and made it easy for later generations to reinterpret these expressions.

In Christian literature, Jesus is invariably referred to as Lord with the understanding, or assumption, that the reader recognizes this compellation as a synonym for God, even though the term itself does not explicitly denote divinity. In the English language, the word "Lord" is not only used in reference to God, but often signifies a human male who operates from a position of authority, such as a British nobleman, a landlord, a drug lord, or a warlord. Similarly, in both the Hebrew Bible and the Greek manuscripts of the New Testament, the word "Lord" is applied to a variety of biblical personages, including God and Jesus.

The Hebrew term *Adon*, which translates to the English "lord," is used in the Old Testament, together with the pronominal suffix *Yod* (similar to the letter "Y"), in reference to God (Exod. 4:13), angels (Zech. 6:4), kings (1 Sam. 26:17), prophets (2 Kings 2:19), fathers (Gen. 31:35), brothers (Gen. 32:5), and even servants (Gen. 24:18). When used in reference to God, however, the form of the word changes slightly from *Adoni* to *Adonai*. This distinction, however subtle, is absolute. No matter where these words appear in the Hebrew Bible *Adonai* always means God, while *Adoni* means anyone, or anything, other than God.

In most English translations of the Bible *Adoni* is written as "lord," with a small *l*, while *Adonai* appears as "Lord," and the fully capitalized "LORD," which also appears in these texts, corresponds to a completely different word that exists only in the Hebrew language. The Tetragrammaton *Yod-Hey-Vav-Hey*, commonly transliterated: YHWH, is believed to be the proper name for God, and, although it is often pronounced *Yahweh,* or *Jehovah,* in Christian circles, in Jewish tradition it is not appropriate, and even forbidden to verbalize these letters; and so, in the English language versions of the Bible the term is rendered as "LORD" to reflect the meaning of the word used in its place during formal recitation of the Bible in the Hebrew language, viz, *Adonai.*

In the New Testament the Greek word *kurios* is used, as with the Hebrew *Adon*, to represent both worldly lords and references to God, however, no distinction is made in the Greek text to differentiate between the two, via capital letters, or otherwise. In the Gospel according to Matthew, for example, when Jesus quotes the following passage from Hebrew scripture, the sacred *Yahweh* is unceremoniously replaced with the small-case form of *kurios*:

> Ye shall not tempt the LORD (*Yahweh*) your God. (Deut. 6:16, KJV)

> It is written again, Thou shalt not tempt the Lord (*kurios*) thy God. (Matt. 4:7, KJV)

Even when the term *kurios* is used as part of Jesus's title, the small-case form of the word appears in most critical versions of the Greek manuscripts.[1]

When translated into English the term *kurios* is almost invariably written as either "Lord," or "LORD," unless the reference being made is to someone other than God or Jesus; and only then is the small case "lord" employed. Consequently, the only way to differentiate between references to God and references to Jesus in the Christian canon is to examine the context of the passage or to look for concordance of related terms and phrases in other parts of the Bible. In the Gospel according to Matthew, for example, when an "angel of the LORD" appears to Joseph (Matt. 1:20), it is obvious that the *kurios* in this case is God because "angel of the LORD" is an expression that occurs frequently in Hebrew scripture as a reference to *Yahweh*, the God of Israel. On the other hand, when Jesus reportedly tells his disciples: "Watch therefore: for ye know not what hour your Lord doth come" (Matt. 24:42, KJV), it is apparent from

---

[1]   See the "Textus Receptus" or Tischendorf's Greek New Testament.

the context of the passage that the Lord in this verse is Jesus because in a subsequent verse the same point is reiterated using the eschatological title, "Son of Man," which belongs exclusively to Jesus in the New Testament:

> Therefore be ye also ready: for in such an hour as ye think not the Son of man cometh. (Matt. 24:44, KJV)

Throughout the New Testament the context of the passage, in most cases, reveals which lord, God or Jesus, was intended by the author, although there are verses in which the identity of the *kurios* is not entirely clear; a prime example of which occurs at the end of the fourth Gospel when Jesus presents his wounds to Thomas, who had refused to believe in the stories of his master appearing to the disciples after the Crucifixion (John 20:24–25). When Thomas reportedly sees the wounds that Jesus allegedly sustained as a result of the Crucifixion, he says to him, "My Lord and my God!" (John 20:28, KJV) in what would seem to be an admission of faith directed at Jesus, although there is no hard evidence in the context of the passage to confirm such an interpretation, nor is there any evidence there to refute it.

From a Muslim perspective this passage could not be authentic because, according to the Koran,[1] Jesus was never crucified in the first place. To the authors of the New Testament, however, the Crucifixion was very real. They believed that the suffering of the Messiah, the Crucifixion

---

[1]   According to the Koran, although it appeared as though Jesus was crucified, he was actually "raised up" (*rafa'a*) to Allah (God) instead. See An-Nisaa: 157–158.

and resurrection, are all events that were prophesied in the Torah and the scripture and that the Crucifixion of Christ was a necessary means to salvation. They praised Jesus for his piety and steadfastness in the face of persecution and admired him for achieving such a close relationship with God, but never did they confuse him with the Almighty. To illustrate this point we need only go back eleven verses from Thomas's statement, where Jesus says to Mary of Magdalene, who was visiting the tomb of her lord after the Crucifixion, "Touch me not; for I am not yet ascended to my Father: but go to my brethren, and say unto them, I ascend unto my Father, and your Father; and to *my God, and your God*" (John 20:17, KJV).

The appearance of these verses, not only in the same gospel, but also in the same chapter, makes it difficult to accept the inclination that Thomas was referring to Jesus when he said, "My Lord and my God" (John 20:28, above), and thus, leaves the objective reader yearning for a more copasetic explanation. Considering the fact that the authors of the New Testament consistently attributed the resurrection of Jesus to God[1] it would seem reasonable to submit that, to the author of the fourth Gospel, Thomas was simply crying out to his God over the excitement of seeing Jesus alive when he exclaimed: "My Lord and my God!" Throughout the gospel narratives when people witnessed miracles performed by Jesus they almost invariably praised God and not Jesus. In the third Gospel, for example, when Jesus heals a paralytic, Luke narrates: "They were all amazed, and they glorified God" (Luke 5:26, KJV). If we assume then, for the sake

---

[1]   Rom. 6:4, Col. 2:12–13, Acts 3:15.

of argument, that Thomas had seen the wounds of Jesus as reported in the fourth Gospel, we must also assume that Thomas was glorifying God and not Jesus when he said: "My Lord and my God!"

Often in the New Testament Jesus is identified as *Lord* and *Christ* in contrast with God the Father, as in the following example, which appears, at least in essence, at the beginning of every epistle attributed to Paul:[1]

> Grace to you and peace from God our Father,
> AND[2] the Lord Jesus Christ. (Rom. 1:7, KJV)

In this way Paul makes it abundantly clear that, although Jesus was indeed his "Lord," he was not his God, and in his letter to the Ephesians the evangelist even adds: "Blessed be *the God* and Father *of our Lord* Jesus Christ" (Eph. 1:3, KJV).

Similar distinctions between God and Jesus can be found throughout the Christian canon, even though both are referred to as Lord. In the Gospel according to Luke, for example, when seventy-two disciples return from a mission of spreading the Gospel and healing the sick, Jesus supplicates to God, saying: "I thank thee, O Father, *Lord of heaven and earth*" (Luke 10:21, KJV), while in the Gospel according to John, when the prophet finishes washing the feet of his disciples, he refers to himself simply as "Lord and the Teacher" (John 13:14, ASV). Only God, "the Father" is described in the Bible as "Lord of heaven and earth." Jesus,

---

[1]   See also 1 Peter 1:3, 2 John 1:3, James 1:1, and Jude 1:1.

[2]   Emphasis added.

on the other hand, is almost invariably defined in human terms.

In the book of Acts, after Jesus is mysteriously separated from his disciples, Peter gives a speech to the Jews in Jerusalem in which several important passages from the Hebrew scripture are quoted. The speech is prompted by the dubious event known as the "coming" of the Holy Spirit, in which "tongues like as of fire" descend from heaven, enabling the disciples to declare "the wonderful works of God" in different languages (Acts 2:1–13, KJV). Peter explains during the speech that this event was foretold in the prophetic writing of Joel and then proceeds to quote the relevant verses (Acts 2:16–21).

Joel warned his people, as did other Israelite prophets, of the coming of the "day of the LORD," an apocalyptic event in which many people would be punished as a result of their iniquities, including a large constituency from among the Children of Israel (Joel 2). In one passage Joel, speaking for God, says: "I will pour out my spirit upon all flesh; and your sons and your daughters shall prophesy" (Joel 2:28, KJV). This *pouring out* of God's spirit onto the righteous remnant of Israel is a common messianic prophecy in the Old Testament, which Peter presumably saw fulfilled in the descent of the "tongues like as of fire" onto the disciples during the Pentecost.

In the same passage Joel, again speaking for God, says: "I will show wonders in the heavens and in the earth" (Joel 2:30, ASV), and these "wonders," according to Peter, were performed by God through Jesus as a sign of his prophethood:

> Ye men of Israel, hear these words; Jesus of
> Nazareth, a *man approved of God* among
> you by miracles and wonders and *signs,*
> *which God did* by him in the midst of you,
> as ye yourselves also know. (Acts 2:22, KJV)

In referring to Jesus as a "man approved of God" Peter effectively removes any and all doubt about how he viewed Jesus in relation to *Yahweh*, the LORD of Joel's prophecy. In fact, Peter makes no attempt whatsoever to connect Jesus to the prophecy except to identify him as the man through which God showed his wonders. Even when Joel says, "whosoever shall call on the name of the Lord shall be saved" (Acts 2:21, KJV), Peter is careful to leave Jesus out of the equation, so to speak.

After declaring Jesus to be a "man approved of God" Peter admonishes the Jews for having him killed and then makes another distinction between God and Jesus, purporting that "God hath raised up" Jesus from the dead (Acts 2:24, KJV).

The resurrection of Jesus, according to Peter, was foretold by David, who presumably writes in the Hebrew Psalter, "I have set the LORD always before me: because he is at my right hand... Therefore my heart is glad... my flesh also shall rest in hope. For thou wilt not leave my soul in hell; neither wilt thou suffer thine Holy One to see corruption" (Ps. 16:8–10, KJV).

Peter reasons that since David was not raised from the dead, whereas Jesus allegedly was, the speaker in the Psalm should be understood as Christ (Acts 2:29–32), which means

Jesus, in Peter's view, worshipped *Yahweh* just like David, before him.

"For David is not ascended into the heavens," Peter continues, "but he saith himself, *The LORD said unto my Lord*, Sit thou on my right hand, Until I make thy foes thy footstool" (Acts 2:34–35, KJV).

These words, which Peter attributes to David, appear as the opening verse of Psalm 110. In the Synoptic Gospels[1] Jesus not only attributes the psalm to David, he portrays it as a messianic prophecy, thereby making himself the second lord that appears in the verse. It's not surprising then that most English translations of the Bible render the beginning of Psalm 110 as "The LORD said to my Lord," or something similar. Such translations, however, are not only misleading, they deviate from the standard convention of using *lord* in places where *Adoni* appears in the Hebrew text and *Lord* when the word *Adonai* is used.

In the Hebrew scripture from whence Peter was quoting, the first lord in Psalm 110 is *Yahweh,* while the second lord is *Adoni.* The word *Adoni* (literally, *my lord*) signifies a human lord, and, indeed, this is the only interpretation that fits the context of the passage. The idea of having *Yahweh,* the God of Israel, address David's Lord, who is also *Yahweh*, is absurd, to say the least, but that's exactly what's implied when the word *Adoni* is translated as "Lord" (with a capital *L*).

---

[1]   See Matt. 22:41–45, Mark 12:35–37, and Luke 20:41–44.

Peter's speech reaches its climax when the disciple proclaims: "Let all the house of Israel know assuredly, that God hath made that same Jesus, whom ye have crucified, both *Lord and Christ*" (Acts 2:36, KJV).

By "Lord," of course, Peter means *Adoni*, the worldly lord in Psalm 110 from which he recites just prior to making this exhortation. Peter would have sounded ridiculous implying that God made Jesus God. Moreover, the lord in this verse could not be God because then that would mean Peter was trying to make Jesus both God and God's anointed, or Messiah.

The worldly lord in Psalm 110, according to Christian scholars, is the Messiah, and the Messiah by all accounts is a man. In the New Testament the humanity of the Messiah is made abundantly clear in one verse, which incidentally is also based on a passage from the Hebrew Psalter. In the opening chapter of Hebrews, while making a comparison between "the Son" (of God) and the angels, the author of the epistle quotes the following verses from Psalm 45:

> But of the Son he saith, *Thy throne, O God, is for ever and ever*; And the sceptre of uprightness is the sceptre of thy kingdom. Thou hast loved righteousness, and hated iniquity; Therefore *God, thy God, hath anointed thee* with the oil of gladness above thy fellows. (Heb. 1:8–9, ASV)

Psalm 45 is one of many psalms that are addressed to the king of Israel as an expression of praise. According to contemporary biblical exegesis the hymn was originally composed in commemoration of a royal wedding, in which the "daughter of Tyre" is encouraged to "consider, and incline thine ear; Forget also thine own people, and thy father's house: So will the king desire thy beauty; For *he is thy lord*; and reverence thou him" (Ps. 45:10–12, ASV). So great was the praise commanded of the king that even his new bride, herself a princess (Ps. 45:13), was expected to bow to him. The author of Hebrews apparently saw a messianic meaning in verse 6 of the psalm (Heb. 1:8), where the speaker reiterates the promises made to David regarding the duration of his throne, and in verse 7 (Heb. 1:9), where the king's anointing is reaffirmed.

Although the Hebrew word *elohim* (god) is commonly used to signify the one supreme god, *Yahweh*, it is also used in the Old Testament in reference to angels, false gods, and judges.[1] In Psalm 45, verse 6, it is used of the Israelite king and, thus, in the context of the Hebrews passage, the Messiah. There can be no doubt, however, that neither the Messiah nor the king of Israel was believed to be divine because in the very next verse (Psalm 45:7, Hebrews 1:9) he is said to have been anointed by his God:

> Thou lovest righteousness, and hatest wickedness: therefore *God, thy God, hath anointed thee* with the oil of gladness above thy fellows. (Ps. 45:7, KJV)

> Thou hast loved righteousness, and hated iniquity; therefore *God, even thy God, hath*

---

[1]   See Psalm 8:5 and Exodus 21:6.

> *anointed thee* with the oil of gladness above
> thy fellows. (Heb. 1:9 KJV)

In the gospel narratives Jesus is identified more frequently as the Messiah, or "Son of God," but is also portrayed as the King of Israel.[1] Either of these titles would have earned him the right to be addressed as "Lord" (in the worldly sense) by his contemporaries, and to the early evangelists both were important.

In the Koran, Jesus is neither a lord nor a king, but rather, a messenger and servant appointed by God; and only Allah (God) is referred to as Lord. In one verse Jesus is said to have referred to God as "my Lord and your Lord" (Al-Maidah:72), just as at the end of the fourth Gospel he refers to the Almighty as "my God, and your God" (John 20:17, KJV). In this way the Koran confirms the Bible, while correcting the misuse of this term.

As the humbleness of Jesus portrayed throughout the Bible suggests he was not interested in becoming *a* lord, his concern was with serving *the* Lord and teaching others to do likewise.

---

[1]   See Luke 19:38, Matt. 21:4–5, John 12:14–15, and John 1:49.

CHAPTER 3

True God and True Man

The fact that the humanity of Jesus is firmly established in the Bible is one point that Muslims and Christians can easily agree upon. We know, for example, that Jesus came into the world, like any other human being, through the womb of his mother (Matt. 1:18–25), that he ate food (Luke 24:41) and required sleep (Matt. 8:24–25), and that he allegedly suffered and died on the cross (Mark 15:15–37), something that God would certainly not be subjected to. After the Crucifixion, according to Paul (Rom. 10:9) and others, Jesus was raised from the dead by God and, according to Luke, continued to require nourishment (Luke 24:41–43). We also learn from the Christian canon that Jesus prayed to God (Matt. 14:23), was dependent on God (John 5:30), and lacked the knowledge of God (Matt. 24:36–37). The significance of these verses, however, is downplayed by Christian apologists, who reason that, because Jesus was both "true God" and "true man," he sometimes needed to emphasize his humanity as well as his divinity.

The problem with this rationale is that it can only be used to reconcile those verses that deal solely with the humanity of Jesus, such as his need for food or the fact that he slept; it provides no explanation as to why Jesus so often expressed subordination to the Father, nor does it account for the fact that the Jews were a learned nation before Jesus came to them.

As members of the Jewish community the disciples undoubtedly knew the difference between God and man, as blasphemy to them was a punishable offense. There would have been no point, therefore, in Jesus telling his disciples: "my Father is greater than I" (John 14:28, KJV), as reported in the fourth Gospel, unless he was intending to emphasize his inferiority to God in a general sense. The setting for this passage is toward the end of Christ's ministry, just prior to the Crucifixion, in what would be the last time the prophet spoke to his disciples until after the resurrection. According to all four Gospel narratives Jesus knew that he would be leaving his disciples soon, and so it's hardly reasonable to imagine—if Jesus was only referring to his humanity—that he would have used this valuable time to teach them something they already knew.

After the Crucifixion, when Jesus refers to the "Father" as "my God" (John 20:17), it becomes eminently clear that, in John's view (or whoever wrote the fourth Gospel), the "Son" had only one nature, viz, that of a man.

The so-called "Fathers of the Church" undoubtedly struggled with such verses, as they desperately wanted to believe that Jesus was God but could not deny the fact that he was human. The solution to this dilemma seemed obvious enough, but it was not until 451CE at the Council of Chalcedon (more than four hundred years after the

Ascension) that Christ was officially declared to have two natures, one human, and one divine.

The authors of the New Testament make it abundantly clear that, in their view, Jesus was always a true man, not only during the days of his ministry, but long after his departure from the world. In Acts of the Apostles, for example, Luke relates to us a speech that was allegedly given by Peter after the Ascension, in which the disciple proclaims to the Israelites that Jesus was "*a man*[1] *approved of God* among you by miracles and wonders and signs, which God did by him in the midst of you" (Acts 2:22, KJV).

Not only does Peter refer to Jesus as a man, he makes a clear distinction between God and Jesus, indicating that even after he had been taken up to heaven, or as Luke puts it, "being by the right hand of God exalted" (Acts 2:33, KJV), the disciple continued to regard Jesus as a human being and God as a separate entity. If Peter had indeed believed that Jesus was "true God and true man," we should expect to see some mention of his divinity here as well as his humanity, but all we have is a proclamation of his humanity.

Luke, of course, was not the only evangelist to contribute to the New Testament, although he is responsible for two of the most important books in the Christian canon. He is the author of record for the Gospel bearing his name and what some refer to as the fifth Gospel, Acts of the Apostles. Saul of Tarsus, a.k.a. Saint Paul, is perhaps the

---

[1]   The word that appears in the Greek text (*aner*) signifies the male sex, and more specifically, an adult male.

most important author of the New Testament, because it is from his letters that the church derives most of its doctrines, particularly in regard to the issue of salvation. Paul is also the greatest contributor to the Christian canon in terms of volume, and his writings are generally believed to represent the earliest portions of the New Testament. In his first letter to Timothy, Paul writes: "For there is one God, and one mediator between God and men, *the man Christ Jesus*" (1 Tim. 2:5, KJV). In line with Peter, speaking through Luke, Paul mentions only the humanity of Jesus and distinguishes him from the Almighty. Paul wrote all of his epistles long after the Ascension of Jesus as he preached to the Gentiles, and, although he claimed to have been appointed an apostle by both God and Jesus (Gal. 1:1), the man who many believe to be the founder of Christianity never confused Jesus with God.

In the Gospel narratives, while Jesus was proclaiming the "kingdom of God" to his people, he reportedly performed great miracles, which for an evangelist harboring the belief that Jesus was both God and man would have undoubtedly been a perfect opportunity to declare the divinity of Jesus. We read, however, in the synoptic Gospels, that the people who witnessed these miracles attributed them to God and not Jesus. In the Gospel according to Luke, for instance, when Jesus heals a paralyzed man in front of a crowd of people, the evangelist writes: "They were all amazed, and they glorified God" (Luke 5:26, KJV). Luke does not mention anything afterward about the ignorance of the people, or that they did not understand that Jesus was really God; he simply moves on to the next topic.

In his version of the same incident, Matthew not only attributes the miracle to God, he adds that the power to perform miracles was given to Jesus by God:

> But when the multitudes saw it, they marvelled, and glorified God, which had given such power unto men. (Matt. 9:8, KJV)

The author of the fourth Gospel is silent about the crowd's glorification of God after witnessing these miracles; although in one incident the evangelist indicates that, in reaction to the multiplication of loaves miracle, the witnesses declared their belief in the prophethood of Jesus:

> Then those men, when they had seen the miracle that Jesus did, said, This is of a truth that prophet that should come into the world. (John 6:14, KJV)

It seems reasonable to assume that if these witnesses, including John, thought that Jesus was "true God and true man," they would have been more concerned about proclaiming their belief in the divinity of Jesus, rather than his prophethood. Prophethood is yet another example of a human characteristic ascribed to Jesus in the Christian canon, where there is seemingly no end to the verses that depict him as a true man, and virtually nothing that portrays him as true God.

The *Parousia,* or second "coming" of Christ, is described in the New Testament as a time of glory for Jesus; a time when the everlasting "kingdom of God" would be fully realized and Jesus would reign with his Father forever and ever. If the early evangelists, therefore, had any reason or desire to proclaim the divinity of Jesus, they would surely have done so while relating these events.

In the synoptic Gospels the return of Jesus coincides with the coming of the "Son of Man," an ambiguous appellation that occurs frequently in the Gospel narratives, although usually from the mouth of Jesus, and, despite the fact that he refers to this mysterious biblical figure consistently in the third person, it is clear in most cases, from the context of the passage, that the prophet assumes this title for himself. In one passage, for example, after asking his disciples, "Who do men say that the Son of man is," Jesus follows with: "Who say ye that I am?" (Matt. 16:13–15, ASV), while in another passage, when Judas comes to identify his former master to the arresting mob, Jesus asks: "Judas, betrayest thou the Son of man with a kiss" (Luke 22:48, KJV)?

Among Christian scholars there is little consensus as to why Jesus adopts this name for himself. Some suggest that it may have messianic implications, while others believe that the expression was used to assert the humanity of Jesus.

The Hebrew expression *ben adam,* which means "son of man," occurs sporadically in the Old Testament, with the exception of Ezekiel, where the term is applied frequently to the prophet for whom the book is named. In most cases the expression is used to symbolize the lowness of man in contrast to the greatness of God, although in one verse it is used of the Davidic king:

> Let thy hand be upon the man of thy right
> hand, upon the son of man whom thou
> madest strong for thyself. (Ps. 80:17, KJV)

The Aramaic equivalent of *ben adam* appears once in the Hebrew Bible, in the book of Daniel, where the prophet describes a vision in which "*one like the Son of man* came with the clouds of heaven" (Dan. 7:13, KJV). In the synoptic Gospels, while explaining to his disciples what would happen after he is gone, Jesus uses these very same words in relation to the *Parousia*:

> Immediately after the tribulation of those days
> shall the sun be darkened, and the moon shall
> not give her light, and the stars shall fall from
> heaven, and the powers of the heavens shall
> be shaken: And then shall appear the sign of
> the Son of man in heaven: and then shall all
> the tribes of the earth mourn, and they shall
> see *the Son of man coming in the clouds of
> heaven* with power and great glory. (Matt.
> 24:29–30, KJV)

The "Son of man" in Daniel's dream appears after four beasts, representing either four kings or four kingdoms (opinions vary), are given authority to rule for a period of time, or until the "Ancient of days" comes and establishes judgment (See Dan. 7:1–14). *Ancient of days* is an expression found only in the writing of Daniel and is generally acknowledged to be a reference to God, while the Son of man is believed to be an allusion to the Messiah. Some scholars suggest that the Son of man in Daniel's dream is a representation of the righteous kingdom that would remain after the final judgment, but in either case it is clear that the Son of man is not God because when the Son of man comes he is "brought near" the Ancient of days and then *given* everlasting dominion over "all people, nations, and languages" (Dan. 7:13–14, KJV), which means not only that the Son of man and the Ancient of days are two distinct beings, but that the Son of man is subordinate to the Ancient of days; and if the Son of man in Daniel's dream is not God then neither is the Son of man of the gospel narratives.

In the book of Revelation, a letter that deals almost exclusively with eschatological events, "John" (the author of record) echoes the words attributed to Jesus by the other evangelists:

> *Behold, he cometh with clouds*; and every eye shall see him. (Rev. 1:7, KJV)

> And I looked, and behold a white cloud, and upon the cloud *one sat like unto the Son of man.* (Rev. 14:14, KJV)

The fact that John regarded Jesus as a true man, and nothing more, is evident from the manner in which he refers to Jesus throughout his so-called revelation. In the opening chapter of the book, for example, the seer declares that Jesus "made us to be a kingdom, to be priests unto *his God* and Father" (Rev. 1:6, ASV), while in another passage John, quoting the Jesus of his vision, writes: "I have found no works of thine perfected before *my God*" (Rev. 3:2, ASV). Wherever God and Jesus are mentioned together in John's apocalypse, Jesus is always portrayed in subordinate terms through expressions like "of God **and** of the Lamb" (Rev.

22:3, KJV), "the Lord God Almighty **and** the Lamb" (Rev. 21:22, KJV), or "of our Lord, **and** of his Christ" (Rev. 11:15, KJV). In fact, even the format of John's letter reveals a certain hierarchy that begins with God and then filters down through Jesus and the angel to John:

> The Revelation of Jesus Christ, which God gave unto him, to shew unto his servants things which must shortly come to pass; and he sent and signified it by his angel unto his servant John: Who bare record of the word of God, and of the testimony of Jesus Christ, and of all things that he saw. (Rev. 1:1–2, KJV)

At no point in John's apocalypse is Jesus portrayed as God; nor is his role in the establishment of the everlasting kingdom conflated with the role of God. Even after defeating the beast[1] and the false prophet who misled people into believing that the beast was worthy of worship, Jesus reigns over the kingdom for only a "thousand" years[2] (Rev. 19:19–20:6), and it's not until after the devil is destroyed (presumably by angels) that God comes into the picture, on a "great white throne" to judge all who had been dead (Rev. 20:11–15, KJV).

Although Paul does not refer to Jesus as "Son of Man" anywhere in his epistles, in his first letter to the Corinthians

---

[1]   Probably borrowed from Daniel 7; possibly a reference to the Roman Empire.

[2]   An arbitrary figure is given to the length of time that Jesus would rule. Jesus would be joined during this reign by the resurrected souls of those who had been martyred for their testimony of Christ (Rev. 20:4).

he does portray Jesus, like John, as a servant of God at the time of judgment.

In one verse Paul describes his savior as the "firstfruits of them that slept (died)" and then declares: "For since by man came death, ***by man*** *came also the resurrection of the dead. For as in Adam all die, even so in Christ shall all be made alive*" (1 Cor. 15:20–22, KJV).

"Firstfruits" is an Old Testament term that refers to the earliest portion of the agricultural harvest, which was offered up to God in accordance with the Law of Moses; however, in the New Testament it refers to the blood sacrifice that was allegedly made by Jesus and, thus, depicts him as an integral part of the human race.

"Then cometh the end," Paul continues, "when he shall have delivered up the kingdom to God, even the Father; when he shall have put down all rule and all authority and power. For he must reign, till he hath put all enemies under his feet" (1 Cor. 15:24–25, KJV). Just as John had quantified the reign of Jesus to a "thousand" years (Rev. 19, above), Paul implies that at some point the Messiah would relinquish power over the kingdom and hand over the reins to God.

When Paul says, "till he hath put all enemies under his feet," he is quoting from Psalm 110, an important messianic prophecy referenced throughout the New Testament, in which the king of Israel is guaranteed divine help and victory. Like many of the early evangelists, Paul saw a connection between Jesus and King David, for whom the psalm was originally composed, and thus, undoubtedly regarded Jesus as little more than a human ruler empowered by God. In fact, as the passage continues, Paul makes it a point to emphasize the subordination of Jesus in relation to God:

> But when he saith all things are put under him, it is manifest that he (God) is excepted, which did put all things under him (Jesus). And when all things shall be subdued unto him (Jesus), *then shall the Son also himself be subject unto him* (God) that put all things under him (Jesus). (1 Cor. 15:27–28, KJV)

The idea of Jesus being made subject to God at the establishment of the kingdom implies that he would not be, even at that time, equal to God. Moreover, the fact that these early evangelists describe Jesus as a distinct being, completely separate from God, at the culmination of his mission indicates clearly that they regarded him as nothing more than a human being. As the Bible clearly states, Jesus was indeed a true man. Therefore, he could not be, from a logical standpoint, true God at the same time because a true man, by the very definition, implies a lack of divinity. When Jesus says, in the Gospel according to Luke, "none is good, save one, that is, God" (Luke 18:19, KJV); he includes himself, and thus, not only affirms his humanity, but his lack of divinity as well.

CHAPTER 4

Seeing Is Believing

Among all the distinctions made between God and Jesus in the Christian canon few are as tangible and readily discernible as the fact that, while Jesus was seen, God could not be. This point is made abundantly clear in the opening chapter of the fourth Gospel, where it is declared in no uncertain terms that "no man hath seen God at any time" (John 1:18, KJV). The only exception to this would be the incident in the desert in which Moses was reportedly permitted to see the back of *Yahweh* after he passed by on top the Mountain of Sinai.[1]

The ability to see God is something people have longed for throughout history, and certainly the disciples of Jesus were no different. Their desire to see God is exemplified in the Gospel according to John, where Jesus reportedly tells his disciples that if they were to follow his commandments and adhere to what he taught they would have a home in heaven, or as the "Son" allegedly puts it, "in my Father's house" (John 14:1–4).

---

[1]   See Exod. 33:18–34:6. See also Exod. 24:9–11, where Moses, Aaron, and the elders of Israel behold the feet of God.

On hearing this, Thomas, who presumably did not understand what Jesus was saying, exclaims: "Lord, we know not whither thou goest; and how can we know the way" (John 14:5, KJV)? Thomas apparently did not realize that Jesus was speaking metaphorically when he said: "Whither I go, ye know the way" (John 14:4, ASV) in the preceding verse.

In response to Thomas, Jesus explains to his disciples that he was in fact the way to the "Father," and thus, indirectly implies that it was to the Father that he was going, and that, because the disciples knew him they knew the "Father" as well and, therefore, the way to meet him:

> I am the way, the truth, and the life: no man cometh unto the Father, but by me. If ye had known me, ye should have known my Father also: and from henceforth ye know him, and have seen him. (John 14:6–7, KJV)

These words, although popular among Christian clergy, do little to alleviate the confusion that the disciples apparently had, and so before long Philip replies: "Lord, show us the Father, and it sufficeth us" (John 14:8, KJV). Philip obviously did not take Jesus literally when he said: "henceforth ye know him," meaning the Father, "and have *seen* him" (John 14:7, KJV).

The root word *horao*, translated here as "seen," refers, in general, to bodily sight, but also relates, as with the English word *see*, to perception of the mind. In some verses *horao* means, "See to it," while in others the word is rendered, "take heed."[1] In the Gospel according to Luke the term is used in reference to a vision that was "seen" by Zechariah:

> And when he came out, he could not speak unto them: and they perceived that he had *seen* a vision in the temple: for he beckoned unto them, and remained speechless. (Luke 1:22, KJV)

Judging from the response that Jesus gives to Philip, it would seem that he did not intend for the word *horao* to be taken literally either in his response to Thomas—"henceforth ye know him, and have *seen* him" (John 14:7, above). When Philip says, "Show us the Father" in verse 8 Jesus does not tell him to have his eyes checked, or try to cure him from blindness; he simply asks the disciple: "hast thou not KNOWN[2] me, Philip" (John 14:9, KJV)? He doesn't say, "Hast thou not *seen* me?" He refers back to the *knowledge* of Jesus that Philip had thus far acquired and then, after repeating his previous statement, explains again what he meant:

> Jesus saith unto him, Have I been so long time with you, and yet hast thou not known me, Philip? *he that hath seen me hath seen the Father;* and how sayest thou then, Shew us the Father? Believest thou not that I am in the Father, and the Father in me? the words that I speak unto you I speak not of myself: but the Father that dwelleth in me, he doeth the works. Believe me that *I am in the Father,*

---

[1] Matt. 16:6, 18:10, Mark 8:15, and Luke 12:15.

[2] Emphasis added.

> *and the Father in me*: or else believe me for
> the very works' sake. (John 14:9–11, KJV)

Jesus appeals to Philip's sense of faith in him, explaining that, if he sincerely believed that Jesus was the Messiah, or in the language of the fourth Gospel, that he was sent by the Father, he should accept the fact that God is working through him, in the words that he said and in the works (miracles) that he performed. At the very least he should have been able to believe based on the miracles that he witnessed because these he saw with his own eyes. Philip would have to be satisfied knowing that the "Father" was *in* Jesus, and that knowing and seeing Jesus was as close to the "Father" as he could get.

The idea of the Father dwelling in the body of Jesus is John's way of saying that Jesus is a prophet. Later, in the same narration, after pleading with the "Father" to protect his disciples, Jesus prays that the entire community of believers would be *in* him, as well as *in* the "Father":

> Neither pray I for these alone, but for them also which shall believe on me through their word; That they all may be one; as thou, Father, art in me, and I in thee, that they also may be one in us: that the world may believe that thou hast sent me. And the glory which thou gavest me I have given them; that they may be one, even as we are one: I in them, and thou in me, that they may be made perfect in one; and that the world may know that thou hast sent me, and hast loved them, as thou hast loved me. (John 17:20–23, KJV)

Jesus was first to be "in" the Father because he was a prophet. Those who believed in his message, however, would later enjoy the same status. They would be "in" the Father, just as Jesus was, and loved by the Father, as he was. The disbelieving Jews, on the other hand, would not be "in" the Father because they did not believe in Jesus, nor had they "seen" the Father in the way that the disciples did. They had undoubtedly seen Jesus in the literal sense, but they did not *see* Jesus in the metaphorical sense that the prophet was referring to when he said to Philip: "He that hath seen me hath seen the Father" (John 14:9, KJV).

CHAPTER 5

The Logos (Word)

In the prologue to the fourth Gospel, Jesus is given, in a roundabout way, the inexplicable title of *Logos* ("the Word") and through this title associated with both creation and the Creator. The importance of these verses to the church and to the creed that it professes cannot be overstated, as they contain some of the most potent and viable evidence in support of their theology. A number of concerns, however, regarding the authenticity of the passage have been brought to light in recent years that effectively eliminate the credibility of this evidence, while at the same time; inconsistencies between the context of the passage and the church's view of Jesus have given way to certain questions regarding the traditional interpretation of these verses.

To begin with, John is the only author in the entire Christian canon that uses the term *Logos* as a proper noun, and even his utilization of the word *Logos* as a name is rare. Aside from the two occurrences in the prologue to the fourth Gospel, where Jesus is clearly identified with "the Word," the only other verse in which the term *Logos* is used as a title by John is in the book of Revelation, where Jesus is depicted as a warrior riding on a horse, whose "name is called The Word of God" (Rev. 19:13, KJV). None of these verses, however, are attributed directly to Jesus, and nowhere in the Bible does Jesus refer to himself, or anyone else, as "the Word" or the "Word of God."

Secondly, the entire concept of the *Logos* as an entity from above is undeniably of pagan origin. In ancient Greek philosophy the term *Logos* had been used long before Jesus was born in a variety of ways to explain the creation of the universe, the order of things, and the relationship between God and man. The earliest known use of the term in relation to the cosmos is by the Greek philosopher Heraclitus. It was developed further in the third century BC by philosophers from the Stoic school of thought and then later by Philo Judaeus, a Jewish philosopher from Alexandria and contemporary of Jesus.

Christian scholars generally acknowledge the role that Greek philosophy has undoubtedly played in John's conception of the Word but also believe that the evangelist drew from Old Testament passages in the books of Genesis and Proverbs to form a scriptural foundation for this unprecedented use of the term. Indeed, the relationship between John's prologue and the book of Proverbs is obvious, as we shall see shortly, but the terminology employed by "John" and, to some extent, the theological implications derived from this terminology, are entirely of Greek origin and completely alien to the Hebrew culture in which the message of Jesus was set.

In the book of Genesis the creation of the world is described as a series of events that occurred immediately upon the *word,* or commandment, of God. For instance, when *God said,* "Let there be light," there was light (Gen. 1:3, KJV) and when *God said*, "Let the waters under the heaven be gathered together unto one place, and let the dry land appear," it became so (Gen. 1:9, KJV). This story of creation, as it is called, is reiterated in the book of Psalms, where it is written: "By the word of the LORD were the heavens made" and "For he spake, and it was done" (Ps. 33:6–9, KJV). Elsewhere in the Hebrew Psalter the "word of the Lord" is said to have brought healing[1] and victory[2] to the Israelites, but for the most part the expression is used in the Old Testament in reference to revelation.

In all of these passages the term "word" is used metaphorically to illustrate the power of God to form and manipulate his creation, and in each case it is really the commandment of God that is being depicted. In this sense the *word* of God could be understood as an attribute of God, much like his mercy or his knowledge, and nothing more than an abstract characteristic that we associate with him.

In the prologue to John's Gospel "the Word" is described as a discrete entity that existed at the time of creation and played a vital role in the creation of "all things," a far cry from the "word of the Lord" in the Old Testament:

> In the beginning was the Word, and the Word was with God, and the Word was God. The same was in the beginning with God. All things were made by him; and without him was not any thing made that was made. (John 1:1–3, KJV)

---

[1]   Ps. 107:17–20

[2]   Ps. 147:12–15.

This personification of God's word, while having no basis in the story of Creation, does bear a striking resemblance to the manner in which Wisdom is personified in the book of Proverbs; particularly in chapter eight, where the author opens with the question: "Doth not wisdom cry?" (Proverbs 8:1, KJV), and then proceeds to conduct an imaginary dialog, wherein Wisdom is seen addressing the "sons of man." In one verse Wisdom declares: "The LORD possessed me *in the beginning* of his way, before his works of old" (Proverbs 8:22, KJV), and then later: "While as yet he had not made the earth, nor the fields… When he prepared the heavens, *I was there*" (Prov. 8:26–27, KJV). Thus, we see that the same preexistence attributed to the Word in John's prologue had previously been used in the Hebrew scripture to promote Wisdom as an essential asset possessed by God before the time of creation, which suggests that "John" had, in all likelihood, fashioned his preexisting *Logos* after the personified Wisdom of Proverbs.

The idea of the Word being "with" God at the time of creation (John 1:1, above) implies that the Word, like Wisdom, is something other than God. The Hebrew word *qanani,* used to describe Wisdom as something "possessed" by God (Prov. 8:22, KJV), comes from the root word *qanah*, which could also mean "create." In fact, the word that appears in the Greek Septuagint in place of *qanani* is *ektisen*, from the root word *ktizo*, which points unmistakably to the act or process of creation. Although the word *ktizo* is not used anywhere in the Bible to describe the Word, it is clear that John was alluding to two distinct entities when he said: "the Word was with God."

In stating that the Word "WAS[1] God" (John 1:1) the author implies that at some point the Word ceased to be God, which is not only absurd, but also wildly incongruent with the most basic and universally recognized characteristics associated with God, viz, that he is eternal and that he never ceases to exist. In another Johannine verse God says that he (God) is the Alpha and the Omega, "*which is*, and *which was*, and *which is to come*, the Almighty" (Rev. 1:8, KJV), and so we see that, when referring clearly to God, John specifies all three phases of existence, but when describing the Word he says only that he ***was***. Moreover, if we interpret John's assertion that "the Word was God" to mean the Word is God; we're left with a verse that contradicts itself, because the Word cannot literally *be* God and be *with* God at the same time. The only conclusion then that one can logically draw from this is that when John said, "the Word was God," he did not mean it literally. Otherwise, we must assume that the original text was corrupted.

Interestingly enough, in the prologue to the fourth Gospel, John declares not only that the Word was with God at the time of creation, but goes on to say that "All things were made *through* (dia)" the Word and that "without him was not anything made that hath been made" (John 1:3, ASV). We've already seen in the book of Genesis how God created the world through a series of commandments, or words, and so when John tells us here that all things were made "through" the Word it would seem, for all intents and purposes, a relatively innocuous statement. The problem is that some English language versions of the Bible render the

---

[1]   Emphasis added.

Greek term *dia* as "by," instead of "through," which in effect transforms the role of the Word from an instrument *through* which things were created into one who creates.

Although the role of the Word in the process of creation is not entirely clear from reading John's prologue, it is clear that the evangelist modeled this mysterious metaphysical being after the personified Wisdom of the Old Testament, where in the eighth chapter of the book of Proverbs Wisdom is described as a "master workman" (some versions, craftsman) that assisted God at the time of creation:

> When he gave to the sea its bound, That the waters should not transgress his commandment, When he marked out the foundations of the earth; Then I was by him, *as a master workman.* (Prov. 8:29–30, ASV)

In this sense we can understand that the Word, like Wisdom, was simply an instrument *through* which God created the heavens and the earth, and not an integral part of his being. What the author of Proverbs was presumably saying is that God used the wisdom that he possessed (and/or created) when he made the heavens and the earth. The fact that "John" had clearly imported the terminology of this passage suggests that he was also attempting to import the meaning as well.

It should also be noted that the use of masculine pronouns in connection with the Word in John's prologue, as well as the feminine pronouns used to personify Wisdom in the book of Proverbs, is nothing more than a literary convention. It would perhaps be more accurate or appropriate to refer to these abstract entities in the neuter, but then that would greatly detract from the poetic character of the passage. The casual reader of the Christian Bible is liable to associate these masculine pronouns with the person Jesus, but the relationship between Jesus and the Word is obscure at best.

After declaring that all things were made *through* the Word, John explains that *in* the Word was life and, as with the previous verses, it is clear that the source of John's inspiration is the book of Proverbs:

> In him was life; and the life was the light of men. And the light shineth in darkness; and the darkness comprehended it not. (John 1:4–5, KJV)

> *Whoso findeth me (Wisdom) findeth life*, and shall obtain favour of the LORD. (Prov. 8:35, KJV)

Simply put, wisdom is the key to success in the Hereafter. In the New Testament "life" is a code word for salvation, and the way to achieve salvation is to walk in the "light" that was provided by Jesus. John uses the terms *life* and *light* metaphorically throughout his Gospel to describe Jesus as a guiding light, whose teachings provided a way of salvation, or "life." In chapter 5, for example, John puts the following words into the mouth of Jesus:

> Verily, verily, I say unto you, *He that heareth my word, and believeth on him that sent me, hath everlasting life*, and shall not come into condemnation; but is passed from death unto life. (John 5:24, KJV)

The one who sent Jesus, of course, is God, and by "hearing" the word of Jesus it is implied that one would be obliged to obey it. Hence, the requirements outlined for obtaining "everlasting life" in the fourth Gospel are to believe in God and to heed the instruction, or "word," of Jesus. This point is elucidated further in the eighth chapter of John, where the Messiah proclaims: *"I am the light of the world: he that followeth me shall not walk in darkness, but shall have the light of life"* (John 8:12, KJV)

As the prologue continues, John the evangelist shifts the reader's attention to John the Baptist, who is identified as a witness to "the Light" and distinguished from him/it:

> There was a man sent from God, whose name was John. The same came for a witness, to bear witness of the Light, that all men through him might believe. He was not that Light, but was sent to bear witness of that Light. That was the true Light, which lighteth every man that cometh into the world. (John 1:6–9, KJV)

The idea that John the Baptist would even be considered as a possible candidate for the role of "the Light" reveals the author's true perception of this esoteric biblical figure in terms of its nature and, by extension, Jesus. That is to say, he is a mortal being, like John, who shares no divinity with the "Father."

When the focus shifts back to Jesus, John goes on to explain how this guiding light of a prophet, who revealed the word of God, was received while he was "in the world":

> He was in the world, and the world was made through him, and *the world knew him not*. He came unto his own, and they that were *his own received him not*. But as many as received him, to them gave he the right to become children of God, even to them that believe on his name: who were born, not of blood, nor of the will of the flesh, nor of the will of man, but of God. (John 1:10–13, ASV)

When John says, "the world knew him not," it's unlikely that he was talking about Jesus in the literal sense. Relatively speaking, only a handful of people out of the world's population had ever encountered Jesus during his days here on earth. Even Paul, the great apostle to the Gentiles, didn't know him personally. What the evangelist presumably was alluding to is the wisdom with which "the world was made through" and the wisdom that God undoubtedly revealed through Jesus. On the other hand, when John says, "his own received him not," he most certainly does mean Jesus, because this clause refers to a specific group of people, namely the Jews, and his dealings with them. This juxtaposing of Jesus and the personified Word, or Wisdom of God, is present throughout the prologue to the fourth Gospel, and particularly evident in the following verse, where the Word is made, or becomes, flesh:

> And the Word was made (*egeneto*) flesh, and *dwelt* among us, and we beheld his glory, the glory as of the only begotten of the Father, full of grace and truth. (John 1:14, KJV)

Verse 14 is the key to understanding the prologue to John's Gospel, because it is here where the personified Wisdom of Proverbs and the Logos of Greek philosophy merge with the "Son of God." In Jewish tradition it was not uncommon for God to speak through prophets and other righteous people, but to the early evangelists Jesus was more than just an ordinary prophet, he was the Messiah and the Son of God. John apparently saw in Jesus a manifestation of God's infinite wisdom, which he (God) undoubtedly possessed at the time of creation, and redefined this relationship in terms of the *Logos*.

The Greek word *egeneto*, translated here "was made," is the same word used for the creation of the world in verse 3, and so it would seem that John saw the incarnation of the Word as a miraculous event orchestrated by God, and the Word itself as something subject to the process of creation and/or susceptible to change.

In stating that the Word "*dwelt* among us" John seems to imply that this manifestation of God's preexistent wisdom in the person Jesus was analogous to the manifestation of God's glory in the tabernacle, or dwelling, that Moses was instructed to build in the book of Exodus.

In the time of Moses, God's glory was allegedly made visible to the Israelites on two occasions—initially, when "the LORD" descended to the top of Mount Sinai (Exod. 19:9–12), and then later by way of a cloud that covered the tent where the tabernacle and the ark of the covenant were housed (Exod. 40:34–38). Thus, they "beheld" the glory of God as the disciples of Jesus would have beheld the glory of the Word by observing the actions of Jesus and listening to him speak.

The Israelites could not, however, see God himself, only his glory. When the LORD (Jehovah) descended to the top of Mount Sinai, they were not allowed to even touch the base of the mountain, lest they be put to death (Exod. 19:12), and when the glory of the LORD had filled the tabernacle even Moses was not able to enter the tent that surrounded it (Exod. 40:34–35).

To suggest then that this glory of God was present in the body of Jesus, when even the mountain of Sinai "quaked greatly" when the "LORD descended upon it" (Exod. 19:18, KJV), would be to cast aside the relevance of the entire Hebrew Bible, something no early evangelist, much less a disciple of Jesus, would have been prepared to do. It was not the glory of God, however, that the disciples beheld, but rather the glory of the Son of God, or as John calls him, "the only begotten of the Father" (verse 14, above). In fact, John even tells us at the end of his prologue: "No man hath seen God at any time" (John 1:18, KJV).

When Moses asked the LORD (*Yahweh*) to show him his glory, he had hoped to see him face to face, but the LORD said to him: "Thou canst not see my face: for there shall no man see me, and live" (Exod. 33:20, KJV). The LORD did reportedly allow Moses briefly to see his back (Exod. 33:18–23), but the rest of the Israelites were permitted only to see the cloud that hung over the tabernacle, where the LORD "dwelled" among them.

Even this "dwelling" of the LORD, however, at the time of Moses, should not be taken literally because, according to Hebrew scripture, it was not possible for God to literally "dwell" on earth. In the historical books of 1 Kings and 2 Chronicles it is reported that when King Solomon finally built the temple, or house "for the name of the LORD" (1 Kings 8:20, KJV), some five centuries after the construction of the Ark and the original dwelling, he had asked rhetorically in prayer: "will God indeed dwell on the earth? behold, the heaven and heaven of heavens cannot contain thee; how much less this house that I have builded" (1 Kings 8:27, KJV)?[1] The Israelite king undoubtedly knew that he could not possibly build a house for God to live in, literally, and that the true dwelling place of God was in heaven. "Hear thou in heaven thy dwelling place" (1 Kings 8:30, KJV), says the righteous ruler in a subsequent verse, and from the Chronicles account of the same event it is clear that the house Solomon built was merely intended to be a place where the LORD would put his name:

> Have respect therefore to the prayer of thy servant, and to his supplication, O LORD my God, to hearken unto the cry and the prayer which thy servant prayeth before thee: That thine eyes may be open upon this house day and night, upon the place *whereof thou hast said that thou wouldest put thy name there.*
> (2 Chron. 6:19–20, KJV)

According to the book of Revelation, which incidentally is also believed to be the work of John, the beloved disciple,

---

[1]   See also 2 Chron. 6 and Acts 7:47–50.

God will eventually dwell among men (Rev. 21:3) after Jesus reigns on earth for a "thousand" years (see Rev. 20), but even at this time Jesus is distinguished from God by the author and referred to as "the Lamb" in contrast to God.

Compared to Jesus, John the Baptist was a relatively insignificant prophet, or at least that's what he says of himself in all four Gospel narratives. "There cometh one mightier than I after me, the latchet of whose shoes I am not worthy to stoop down and unloose" (Mark 1:7, KJV), says John in each of the three synoptic Gospels, while in the Gospel according to John the Baptist adds that the reason Jesus was superior to him is because "he was before me":

> John bare witness of him, and cried, saying,
> This was he of whom I spake, He that cometh
> after me is preferred before me: for *he was
> before me*.[1] (John 1:15, KJV)

Christian exegesis of this verse is based on the assumption that the Word is simply another appellation for the Son of God, or second person of the "Blessed Trinity," employed as a means to accentuate his role in creation, and so, when John says of the Word, "he was before me," it is believed to be in reference to the "true God" in Jesus as opposed to the "true man." We must remember, however, that it was the glory of the "only begotten of the Father" that the witnesses of Jesus beheld when the Word "dwelt" among them (John 1:14), and not the Father himself. In both the Hebrew Bible as well as the New Testament, the "Father" is consistently equated with *Yahweh*, the God of Israel, while

---

[1]   See also John 1:30.

the Son, or "only begotten of the Father," is identified as the Messiah, and the Messiah, by all accounts, is a mortal being. Therefore, Jesus, as the Messiah, could not have preexisted except in a figurative sense. The Word, on the other hand, which is clearly modeled after the personified Wisdom of Proverbs, is an abstract trait or ideology that undoubtedly existed at the time of creation and certainly before John the Baptist, but John was not comparing himself to an abstract ideology, nor is it plausible that an Israelite prophet would compare himself to God.

If we look closely at the manner in which John compares himself to Jesus in all four of the Gospel narratives, it is clear that the Baptist was alluding to his status in the sight of God versus that of Jesus, essentially conceding that he was a lesser prophet. As the Messiah, Jesus was "mightier" than John (Mark 1:7, KJV) and "preferred before" him (John 1:30, KJV). This point needed to be emphasized in order to promote Jesus as the one anointed by God to restore the kingdom of Israel. It was understood that God was mightier than John.

The fact that John the Baptist was addressing the prophethood of Jesus and not some divine characteristic he perceived of him is reaffirmed in verse 17 of the prologue, when John the evangelist compares Jesus with Moses:

> For the law was given by Moses, but grace and truth came by Jesus Christ. (John 1:17, KJV)

John's confession in the fourth Gospel that Jesus "was before me" could either be a reference to the preexisting *Logos* that had been "made flesh" in verse 14 or an allusion to the alleged resurrection of Jesus. In verse 15 the word that appears in the Greek text corresponding to the English word "before" is *protos,* the superlative form of *pro,* which is the real Greek word for "before." In fact, it is only here in the opening chapter of John's Gospel that the Greek term *protos* is translated as "before." Hence, John was not actually saying that Jesus was "before" him, but rather, that he was "first." Why is this important? Because elsewhere in the New Testament the compound word *prototokos,* meaning "firstborn," is used to describe Jesus, both in terms of his humanity as well as his association with the Logos. In his letter to the Colossians, for example, Paul refers to Jesus, initially, as "the firstborn of all creation," and then, three verses later, as "the firstborn from the dead":

> Who is the image of the invisible God, *the firstborn (prototokos) of all creation*; for in him were all things created, in the heavens and upon the earth, things visible and things invisible, whether thrones or dominions or principalities or powers; all things have been created through him, and unto him; and he is before (*pro*) all things, and in him all things consist. And he is the head of the body, the church: who is the beginning, *the firstborn (prototokos) from the dead*; that in all things he might have the preeminence. (Col. 1:15–18, ASV)

Paul's use of Hellenistic language is not surprising, given the fact that he spent the majority of his Christian life preaching to the Gentiles. It is also possible, however, that these words are not actually his. In the book of Romans, the "crown jewel" of Pauline epistles, Paul uses the same terminology in reference to God, the "Father,"[1] while in his letter to the Ephesians the evangelist attributes creation exclusively to God:

> Unto me, who am less than the least of all saints, was this grace given, to preach unto the Gentiles the unsearchable riches of Christ; and to make all men see what is the dispensation of the mystery which for ages hath been hid in *God who created all things.*[2] (Eph. 3:8–9, ASV)

Although Paul is the only evangelist to designate Jesus (supposedly) as the "firstborn of (all) creation," both he and John refer to the Messiah as "firstborn of/from the dead,"[3] an expression that clearly depicts Jesus as a mortal being and marks his alleged resurrection as the first of many to come when the so-called messianic age finally comes to fruition. In a related verse, Paul refers to Jesus as the "firstborn among many brethren" (Rom. 8:29, KJV) after declaring that the followers of Christ, or "children of God" (Rom. 8:16, KJV), would be raised from the dead in the same manner that Jesus allegedly was (Rom. 8:11).

In the Old Testament, "firstborn" is a title that was awarded to the oldest son in a family as a token of his birthright.[4]

---

[1]   See Rom. 11:33–36.

[2]   Some ancient manuscripts add "through Christ Jesus" at the end of Eph. 3:9.

[3]   Rev. 1:5, Col. 1:18.

[4]   See Deut. 21:15–17.

The name was also given to Israel in recognition of her status among nations.[1] Here in the New Testament, John and Paul seem to imply that, since Jesus was the first to be "born" into the next life, he has the right of inheritance over all humanity from God, the "Father."

Regardless of what John meant by the expression "firstborn of the dead," or by his testimony on behalf of the Baptist, that Jesus was "before" him, it is clear from the final verse of the prologue that the evangelist did not believe Jesus was God:

> No man hath seen God at any time; the only begotten Son, which is in the bosom of the Father, he hath declared him. (John 1:18, KJV)

In these concluding remarks, John emphasizes one of the most important and fundamental points to ever emerge from the Hebrew scripture, viz, that no one has seen God at any time, including Moses. The concept of an unseen god is what distinguished the Children of Israel from the pagan societies of the ancient world. The fact that Jesus is portrayed as the incarnate Word of God by an early evangelist, who obviously had been influenced by Greek philosophy, does not change the fact that no man has ever seen God. Jesus, identified as "the only begotten Son," is thus distinguished from God and, instead, described as the one who "*declared* God."

---

[1]   Exod. 4:22.

CHAPTER 6

Before Abraham Was …

In the previous chapter we discussed how the author of the fourth Gospel portrayed Jesus as the incarnate form of the *Logos* and how this led to the belief that Jesus himself had in some way existed prior to the creation of "all things." In this chapter we will examine a similar verse that, in its present state, would seem to support the traditional view of Jesus.

The eighth chapter of John's Gospel begins with a story about a woman "taken in adultery" (John 8:3, KJV), which according to *Christian* scholars is not authentic.[1] The evidence for this avouchment lies in the text of the gospel itself and the apparent insertion of the story. In John 7, for example, when Jesus goes to the temple to observe the "feast of tabernacles" (John 7:1–10), all indications are that he remains there through the end of the chapter, and then, at the beginning of the next chapter (John 8), goes to the "mount of Olives" for the adulteress scene (John 8:1). The remainder of John 8, however, seems to be a continuation of events that took place at the temple, and

---

[1] See footnotes in the NIV and New American Bible corresponding to John 7:53—8:11

at the end of the chapter Jesus reportedly leaves the temple (John 8:59). Hence, right from the get-go, we have an issue of authenticity surrounding the chapter, in which Jesus, on three separate occasions, uses the expression "I am" in a way that is perceived by many to be a claim of divinity, or at least an allusion to his alleged preexistence.

After Jesus pardons the adulteress in verse 11 of the narration, the remainder of the chapter involves a dialog between him and the Pharisees, in which the prophet is seen defending his honor and the validity of his message. The Pharisees initially object when Jesus says: "*I am* the light of the world"—not because they didn't believe him, but because he testified on his own behalf (John 8:12–13). When Jesus claims to have a second witness in "the Father that sent me," the Pharisees ask: "Where is thy Father?" (John 8:17–19, KJV), to which, Jesus responds: "Ye neither know me, nor my Father: if ye had known me, ye should have known my Father also" (John 8:19, KJV) and then continues to rebuke them, saying: "Ye are from beneath; I am from above: ye are of this world; I am not of this world… if ye believe not that *I am he*, ye shall die in your sins" (John 8:23–24, KJV).

To the casual reader it may seem as though Jesus was proclaiming divinity for himself when he said, reportedly, "I am not of this world." It should be noted, however, that later in the same Gospel these words are applied to the disciples of Jesus during the requisite "Last Supper" scence.[1] It is also apparent from the context of the passage that this expression is a reiteration of the words "I am from above"

---

[1] See John 17:14.

and, thus, neither expression should be interpreted as a claim of divinity.

The Greek words *egow eimee,* meaning "I am," in verse 24, are often rendered "I am he," with the second pronoun, either in brackets, or italicized to indicate that the "he" is only implied. In some versions of the Bible a connection is drawn between these words attributed to Jesus and the Hebrew word *Ehyeh,* which according to the book of Exodus is an expression that God used in reference to himself after commissioning Moses to lead the Israelites out of Egypt.[1]

Ehyeh is most commonly translated "I am" but could also mean "I will be." It is believed to be related to *Yahweh,* the most sacred and more common name for God in the Hebrew scripture, and Jesus, according to many biblical commentators, was applying this name to himself during his conversation with the Pharisees in the Gospel according to John. From the context of the passage, however, it is clear that Jesus was not claiming to be God, or at least the Pharisees didn't think so, because after being told by Jesus: "if ye believe not that *I am* he, ye shall die in your sins," the Pharisees ask: "Who art thou" (John 8:24–25, KJV)? They do not accuse him of blasphemy.

Christian apologists have tried to explain this by saying that the Pharisees didn't realize what Jesus was telling them; however, John does not mention anything in his narration that would seem to support such an argument. Jesus simply answers their question and tells them that he is "the same

---

[1]   See Exod. 3:13–14.

that I said unto you *from the beginning*" (John 8:25, KJV), and then reemphasizes the fact that he was sent by God, who "is true" (John 8:26, KJV), and this, according to John, is what the Pharisees did not understand. They did not understand that when Jesus was talking about his "Father," or "he that sent me" (John 8:27, KJV), he was referring to God.

What Jesus told the Pharisees in the beginning of the discourse is, "*I am* the light of the world" (John 8:12), and this undoubtedly is what he meant when he said, "if ye believe not that *I am*" in verse 24. In declaring himself to be the "light of the world" Jesus was essentially claiming to be the Messiah. This expression, in all likelihood, is a reference to the servant of the Lord described in Isaiah as a "light of nations" (Isa. 42:6, YLT) and, as the Messiah, or servant of the Lord, Jesus is thus distinguished from God. The idea of Jesus proclaiming to be the Lord, God of Israel to a crowd of disbelieving Jews is unfathomable, to say the least—especially when we consider the fact that in the Gospel according to Matthew, as well as in the Marcan parallel, Jesus did not even want them to know that he was the Messiah:

> Now when Jesus came into the parts of Caesarea Philippi, he asked his disciples, saying, Who do men say that the Son of man is? And they said, Some say John the Baptist; some, Elijah; and others, Jeremiah, or one of the prophets. He saith unto them, But who say ye that I am? And Simon Peter answered and said, Thou art the Christ, the Son of the living God... *Then charged he the disciples*

> *that they should tell no man that he was the*
> *Christ.* (Matt. 16:13–20, ASV)

Realizing that the Pharisees were not willing to acknowledge his relationship with "the Father," Jesus declares: "When ye have *lifted up* the Son of man, then shall ye know that *I am* he, and that I do nothing of myself; but as my Father hath taught me, I speak these things" (John 8:28, KJV). The words "lifted up," which appear in the English translation of this verse, come from the Greek word *hupsoo*, which means, to "exalt" or "raise up." Traditionally this term has been taken literally as a reference to the "lifting up" of Jesus onto the cross,[1] although the exact meaning of the term as it relates to Jesus is difficult to pinpoint. Suffice it to say, for our discussion here, that Jesus was alluding in some way to the events surrounding the Crucifixion. The words "I am," which appear here for the second time in the chapter, refer back to verse 24, where Jesus warned the Pharisees that they would die in their sins if they did not believe that he was the Messiah:

> I said therefore unto you, that ye shall die in
> your sins: for if ye believe not that I am he, ye
> shall die in your sins. (John 8:24, KJV)

The refusal of the Jews to recognize Jesus as the Messiah is one of the primary themes woven throughout each of the four Gospel narratives, and it was this rejection for which Jesus most often rebuked them. Nowhere in the Christian canon does Jesus rebuke the Jews for failing to acknowledge him as God. In verse 28, as well as in the following verse, the

---

[1]   See John 3:1–21.

words attributed to Jesus by John make it profoundly clear that Jesus was not claiming to be God during his dialog with the Pharisees, as he expresses in plain terminology his subordination to God:

> Then said Jesus unto them, When ye have lifted up the Son of man, then shall ye know that I am he, and that *I do nothing of myself*; but as my Father hath taught me, I speak these things. And he that sent me is with me: the Father hath not left me alone; for *I do always those things that please him*. (John 8:28–29, KJV)

As the passage continues, Jesus focuses on a smaller group of Jews who supposedly believed him, saying: "If ye continue in my word, then are ye my disciples indeed; And ye shall know the truth, and the truth shall make you free" (John 8:31–32, KJV). These words, however, do little to convince the new audience, and so before long the prophet is seen accusing them of being children of the devil in a figurative sense.[1]

When the Jews claim that Abraham is their father, Jesus accuses them of trying to kill him and then makes another distinction between God and himself:

> Jesus saith unto them, If ye were Abraham's children, ye would do the works of Abraham. But now ye seek to kill me, a man that hath told you *the truth, which I have heard of God*. (John 8:39–40, KJV)

---

[1]   See John 8:38.

The Jews respond to this by claiming to have God as their father (John 8:41), to which, Jesus replies, "If God were your Father, ye would love me" (John 8:42, KJV) and then goes on to explain that the reason why they could not accept his word, or his message, is because they were not (children) "of God" (John 8:47).

Finally, when the Jews hear Jesus say: "If a man keep my word, he shall never see death," they exclaim: "Abraham died, and the prophets; and thou sayest, If a man keep my word, he shall never taste of death. Art thou greater than our father Abraham" (John 8:51–53, ASV)?

At this point the conversion takes a strange turn and then eventually becomes incoherent. As a teacher and a prophet sent to the Children of Israel, one would expect Jesus to explain what he meant when he said that those who obeyed his word would never see death, if he did in fact utter these words. He obviously didn't mean it literally. Even the "Son of God" himself, according to all four Gospel narratives, had to experience death, and certainly his disciples met the same fate. Unfortunately, Jesus does not explain what he meant; however, he does respond in the following manner to the question raised concerning his status in relation to Abraham:

> Your father Abraham rejoiced to see my day:
> and he saw it, and was glad. (John 8:56, KJV)

The traditional wording of the next verse in John's narration implies that the Jews not only failed to understand the meaning behind these words that Jesus allegedly spoke but also twisted the words in a way that would seem to facilitate the Christian interpretation of the passage:

> Then said the Jews unto him, Thou art not yet
> fifty years old, and hast thou seen Abraham?
> (John 8:57, KJV)

How the Jews supposedly got from Abraham "seeing" Jesus's day to Jesus seeing Abraham is a question that Christian apologists have undoubtedly struggled with for years. Fortunately for them, the answer to this mystery has now been solved through the discovery of older manuscripts that depict the Jews questioning the notion of Abraham "seeing" Jesus in verse 57, rather than Jesus seeing Abraham.[1]

This apparent tampering of the "original" text, both here and at the beginning of the chapter, must be taken into consideration when evaluating the credibility of John's testimony, if an honest approach to understanding the Bible is to be sought, and the fact that John is the only evangelist to report this dialog makes critical analysis even more important. The reason for the emphasis here is because one of the most heavily quoted verses in contemporary Christian literature appears immediately following this corrupted text in what seems to be an unauthentic passage. It is the third occurrence of the expression "I am" and perhaps the most ambiguous of the three:

---

[1]   See corresponding footnotes in the New American Bible, the English Standard Version of the Bible, and the Holman Christian Standard Bible.

> Jesus said unto them, Verily, verily, I say
> unto you, Before Abraham was, *I am*. (John
> 8:58, KJV)

This time Christian scholars are far more unified in their rendition of these words, as virtually every English translation of John 8:58 reads, "I am," without the implied pronoun *he*, and many versions include commentaries that refer the reader to the incident of the burning bush, where God allegedly applies the expression as a name for himself.[1] This, despite all the references that Jesus makes to God in the passage as the one who sent him—the expressions of servitude and submission, the evidence of corruption in John's exclusive account of the dialog, and the implausibility of Jesus making such a statement.

If Jesus had in fact claimed to be God while addressing the Jews in the temple, we should expect to see some mention of it afterward; however, nowhere in the remaining chapters of his Gospel does John make even a casual reference to the incident. At the very least we should expect to see Jesus being charged with claiming to be *Yahweh,* or the Father, during one of his trials, yet nowhere in any of the four Gospel narratives is Jesus formally charged with impersonating the Almighty. According to John, the charge brought against Jesus by the Jews is that he "made himself the Son of God" (John 19:7, KJV), and Son of God, as we have already shown, is an appellation that means nothing more than the Messiah, son of David.

---

[1] Exod. 3.

In Matthew's Gospel, the "chief priests, and elders, and all the council" have difficulty finding witnesses to testify against Jesus until two men step forward and say: "This fellow said, I am able to destroy the temple of God, and to build it in three days" (Matt. 26:59–61, KJV). Jesus, of course, never said that he would demolish the temple. He said that he would raise it up in three days, but that, according to John, the only evangelist to record the incident, was in reference to the resurrection.[1] Based on his reaction to the testimony against Jesus, the high priest does not seem to have interpreted it as a claim of divinity; he simply asks Jesus for his side of the story and, when the prophet refuses to defend himself, demands that Jesus tell him whether or not he is "the Messiah, the Son of God" (Matt. 26:62–63).

In the Gospel according to Mark, when asked, "Art thou the Christ, the Son of the Blessed?" Jesus replies, "*I am*: and ye shall see the Son of man sitting on the right hand of power, and coming in the clouds of heaven" (Mark 14:61–62, KJV). This statement, according to both Mark and Matthew, was viewed as blasphemous by the high priest, but still not a claim of divinity.[2] More importantly, it demonstrates clearly what Jesus meant by the expression "I am," viz, the Messiah, the Son of God.

---

[1] See John 2:19–21.

[2] Mark 14:64–65 and Matt. 26:65–68.

CHAPTER 7

The Alpha and the Omega

There is arguably no book in the entire Bible that stands out more than the book of Revelation. Known for its bizarre and vivid descriptions of events leading up to the Final Judgment, this apocalyptic work of literary art has attracted countless souls throughout the ages seeking knowledge about the future and the destiny of mankind. The final chapter in the Christian canon, Revelation is one of five books attributed to John, the son of Zebedee, and, like the Gospel which bears his name, filled with allegorical language that is difficult to interpret and easily misunderstood, such as the arcane designation Alpha and Omega, which the author uses indiscreetly as a reference to God's omnipotence and obliquely in relation to the return of Jesus.

The words *Alpha* and *Omega*[1] appear for the first time in the opening chapter of John's apocalypse and, although the speaker there is clearly identified as God, most Red

---

[1]   Alpha and Omega, the first and last letters of the Greek alphabet respectively, are spelled out phonetically in some Greek manuscripts, while in other texts only the letters themselves appear.

Letter editions of the Bible present the verse in red type to implicate Jesus as the speaker:

> I am the Alpha and the Omega, saith the
> Lord God, who is and who was and who is
> to come, the Almighty. (Rev. 1:8, ASV)

For many Christians this does not present a problem, since most likely they believe that Jesus is God; however, based on contextual evidence, both within the passage and elsewhere, there is reason to believe that John did not intend for these words to be put into the mouth of Jesus.

The book of Revelation begins by claiming to be "The Revelation of Jesus Christ, which *God gave unto him*" (Rev. 1:1, KJV), a statement which not only depicts Jesus as a separate being, distinct from God, but also indicates that he was dependent on God for the revelation that he allegedly revealed to John. In the next verse John is said to have bared witness to both the "word of God" AND the "testimony of Jesus Christ" (Rev. 1:2, KJV), and so it is reaffirmed that God is the source of this revelation, and that Jesus is but a witness. In his salutation John even refers to Jesus as a "faithful witness," in contrast to God, who he describes as "him who is and who was and who is to come" (Rev. 1:4–5, ASV).

This distinction between "him who is and who was and who is to come" (i.e., God) and Jesus, the "faithful witness," essentially proves that Christ was not the Alpha and the Omega described in verse 8 as the one "who is and who was and who is to come." Moreover, the Alpha and the Omega described in verse 8 is clearly identified as "Lord

God," a designation reserved for *Yahweh* in the Bible and never applied to Jesus. "Lord God," in fact, is the "God and Father" of Jesus alluded to at the end of John's salutation:

> Unto him that loveth us, and loosed us from
> our sins by his blood; and he made us to be
> a kingdom, to be priests unto *his God* and
> Father. (Rev. 1:5–6, ASV)

It is difficult to imagine that John would make such a clear reference to the fact that Jesus has a God in verse 6 if he thought he was the "Lord God" or "the Almighty" described in verse 8. Even from a Christian standpoint this has to be obvious, and thus we see in the Red Letter edition of the Holman Christian Standard Bible that Rev 1:8 is printed in black ink, indicating that those who translated this English version of the Bible did not believe Jesus was the one speaking when John wrote: "I am the Alpha and the Omega, saith the Lord God, who is and who was and who is to come, the Almighty" (Rev. 1:8, ASV).

The second occurrence of the words Alpha and Omega comes near the end of the apocalypse after all the forces of evil—Gog and Magog, the devil, the beast, and the false prophet—have been thoroughly destroyed:

> And he that sat upon the throne said, Behold,
> I make all things new. And he said unto me,
> Write: for these words are true and faithful…
> *I am Alpha and Omega, the beginning and
> the end…* He that overcometh shall inherit
> all things; and I will be his God, and he shall
> be my son. (Rev. 21:5–7, KJV)

This time the speaker is identified as "he that sat upon the throne," an expression allocated to God in the book of Revelation and, consequently, no attempt is made by Christian scholars to attribute these words to Jesus.

John uses the words Alpha and Omega once more in the final chapter of his book and, although the passage seems poorly constructed and difficult to follow, it is evident from the context that the speaker in this case is supposed to be Jesus. It should be noted, however, that, while the evangelist does apparently apply the same expression to Christ that had been previously assigned to *Yahweh*, he is careful not to use the word God in reference to Jesus:

> And, behold, I come quickly; and my reward
> is with me, to give every man according as
> his work shall be. I am Alpha and Omega, the
> beginning and the end, the first and the last.
> (Rev. 22:12–13, KJV)

Exactly what John meant by the words Alpha and Omega is not entirely clear. It does not seem likely that Jesus, who reportedly spoke Aramaic and undoubtedly preached from the Hebrew scripture, would have placed any significance on these letters. In the Hebrew language there is no such thing as an Omega and the last letter of the Hebrew alphabet is *Tav*. Given the evidence of Hellenism in his Gospel, and the fact that *Alpha* and *Omega* are symbols of Greek origin, it would seem reasonable to assume that "John" must have borrowed this terminology from the pagans, like he presumably did with the *Logos*.

In some manuscripts[1] the words Alpha and Omega appear a fourth time at the beginning of Revelation 1:11, which suggests that the original text of John's apocalypse may have been manipulated at some point, perhaps by a copyist. It also helps to explain why the other three verses that contain the words Alpha and Omega seem out of place and incongruent with the context of the passages in which they appear. The first occurrence, for example, appears in between a greeting that John extends to the seven churches and a verse in which he describes the circumstances that led to his vision:

[Revelation 1:4-11, ASV]

4 John to the seven churches that are in Asia: Grace to you and peace, from him who is and who was and who is to come; and from the seven Spirits that are before his throne;

5 and from Jesus Christ, who is the faithful witness, the firstborn of the dead, and the ruler of the kings of the earth. Unto him that loveth us, and loosed us from our sins by his blood;

6 and he made us to be a kingdom, to be priests unto his God and Father; to him be the glory and the dominion for ever and ever. Amen.

---

[1] English versions of the Bible that include the words "Alpha and Omega" in Rev 1:11 are based on the Textus Receptus (received text), which differs at times from some of the most ancient and valued codices.

⁷ Behold, he cometh with the clouds; and every eye shall see him, and they that pierced him; and all the tribes of the earth shall mourn over him. Even so, Amen.

⁸ I am the Alpha and the Omega, saith the Lord God, who is and who was and who is to come, the Almighty.

⁹ I John, your brother and partaker with you in tribulation and kingdom and patience which are in Jesus, was in the isle that is called Patmos, for the word of God and the testimony of Jesus.

¹⁰ I was in the Spirit on the Lord's day, and I heard behind me a great voice, as of a trumpet

¹¹ saying, What thou seest, write in a book and send it to the seven churches....

Notice how the flow of the passage, in which John is the speaker, is suddenly interrupted in verse 8, where God is the speaker, and that this declaration from the "Lord God" has nothing to do with the context of the passage. Similarly, in the second occurrence of the words Alpha and Omega, the same phenomenon can be observed:

[Revelation 21:5-8, KJV]

⁵And he that sat upon the throne said, Behold, I make all things new. And he said unto me, Write: for these words are true and faithful.

⁶And he said unto me, It is done. I am Alpha and Omega, the beginning and the end.

I will give unto him that is athirst of the fountain of the water of life freely.

⁷He that overcometh shall inherit all things; and I will be his God, and he shall be my son.

⁸But the fearful, and unbelieving, and the abominable, and murderers, and whoremongers, and sorcerers, and idolaters, and all liars, shall have their part in the lake which burneth with fire and brimstone: which is the second death.

This time the speaker throughout the passage is God, however—as with the previous example, there doesn't seem to be any relation between the anomalous declaration, "I am the Alpha and the Omega" (Rev. 21:6, ASV), and the remainder of the passage, nor does there seem to be any logical explanation as to why God would suddenly say, "It is done." In fact, if we read the passage without the beginning of verse 6 it seems to make more sense.

The third occurrence of the words Alpha and Omega appears in the epilogue of Revelation, in a passage where the speaker changes at least four times:

[Revelation 22:6-15, KJV]

⁶And he said unto me, These sayings are faithful and true: and the Lord God of the holy prophets sent his angel to shew unto

his servants the things which must shortly be done.

⁷Behold, I come quickly: blessed is he that keepeth the sayings of the prophecy of this book.

⁸And I John saw these things, and heard them. And when I had heard and seen, I fell down to worship before the feet of the angel which shewed me these things.

⁹Then saith he unto me, See thou do it not: for I am thy fellowservant, and of thy brethren the prophets, and of them which keep the sayings of this book: worship God.

¹⁰And he saith unto me, Seal not the sayings of the prophecy of this book: for the time is at hand.

¹¹He that is unjust, let him be unjust still: and he which is filthy, let him be filthy still: and he that is righteous, let him be righteous still: and he that is holy, let him be holy still.

¹²And, behold, I come quickly; and my reward is with me, to give every man according as his work shall be. ¹³I am Alpha and Omega, the beginning and the end, the first and the last.

¹⁴Blessed are they that do his commandments, that they may have right to the tree of life, and may enter in through the gates into the city.

15For without are dogs, and sorcerers, and whoremongers, and murderers, and idolaters, and whosoever loveth and maketh a lie.

The flow of this passage is broken twice by an exclamation from Jesus (verses 7 and 12), the second of which contains the aberrant "Alpha and Omega" (verses 12–13); and in each case the passage seems more coherent without these verses.

The task of decoding the meaning behind the words (or letters) *Alpha* and *Omega* is complicated further by the fact that there is no concordance for this expression in any other part of the Bible, including each of the four other books— one Gospel and three epistles—attributed to John. In fact, nowhere in the Bible besides John's apocalypse is anyone, including God and Jesus, referred to as either "the Alpha and the Omega," or "the Beginning and the End."

In the book of Isaiah the Lord God of Israel refers to himself as "the first and the last,"[1] but, interestingly enough, John reserves this honorary distinction for Jesus, who reportedly appeared to him in a vision as "one like unto the Son of man" with eyes "as a flame of fire," a voice "as the sound of many waters" and a face "as the sun shineth in his (its) strength" (Rev. 1:13–16, KJV). In the same narration John tells us that when he saw this intimidating figure he "fell at his feet as dead" (Rev. 1:17, KJV), and that Jesus, upon seeing this display of humiliation, said: "Fear not; I am *the first and the last*: I am he that liveth, and was dead; and, behold, I am alive for evermore" (Rev. 1:17–18, KJV), as if to

---

[1]   See Isa. 41:4, 44:6, and 48:12.

comfort his disciple by identifying himself. Apparently John thought he had seen God, and Jesus wanted to assure him that he was merely a servant of the Almighty, the one who died on the cross and then rose from the dead (according to the authors of the New Testament), which would make him the *first* to be resurrected. From this we can deduce that the expression "first and last," as it relates to Jesus, has something to do with his death and resurrection, and perhaps the Parousia, but nothing to do with divinity.

CHAPTER 8

Worship

It may be asked—and with good reason—why, if Jesus is not God, was he reportedly worshipped in the Bible? In the Gospel according to Matthew, for instance, when the disciples see Jesus on the mountain in Galilee (Matt. 28:16–17), or in the Gospel according to Luke, when Jesus is "carried up into heaven" (Luke 24:51–52, KJV), why do his disciples reportedly *worship* him?

The answer to this question, if an objective approach is desired, demands an in-depth look at the Greek word *proskuneo* that appears in the ancient manuscripts of the Bible and corresponds to the English word *worship* in numerous verses, many of which seem to portray Jesus as someone worthy of the same worship one would attribute to God.

According to most academic biblical references[1] the Greek word *proskuneo* does not in-and-of itself mean *worship*, but rather, refers to the act of prostration, which in biblical times was performed not only in reverence to God but also out of respect to people of superior stature. The Greek word

---

[1]   See Thayer's *Greek-English Lexicon of the New Testament* or *Vine's Expository Dictionary of New Testament Words*.

proskuneo can be compared with the Hebrew word *shachah*, which describes the act of prostration performed by David in honor of King Saul in the book of Samuel:

> David also arose afterward, and went out of the cave, and cried after Saul, saying, My lord the king. And when Saul looked behind him, *David stooped with his face to the earth, and bowed himself.* (1 Sam. 24:8, KJV)

In the Gospel according to Matthew, the word *proskuneo* is used to describe the action taken by a Canaanite woman as she approaches Jesus for help with her demon-possessed daughter:

> Then Jesus went thence, and departed into the coasts of Tyre and Sidon. And, behold, a woman of Canaan came out of the same coasts, and cried unto him, saying, Have mercy on me, O Lord, thou son of David; my daughter is grievously vexed with a devil. But he answered her not a word. And his disciples came and besought him, saying, Send her away; for she crieth after us. But he answered and said, I am not sent but unto the lost sheep of the house of Israel. *Then came she and worshipped* (proskuneo) *him*, saying, Lord, help me. (Matt. 15:21–25, KJV)

Although translations of the word *proskuneo* in this passage vary from version to version, it is clear that the woman of Canaan was simply prostrating herself to Jesus out of desperation, in an attempt to earn his pity, because it's not until after Jesus rejects her that she "worships" him. In some versions of the Bible the word *proskuneo* in verse 25 (above) is rendered, "knelt before," while in Young's Literal Translation of the Bible the woman is seen "bowing" to Jesus. In other versions, such as our example here from King James, the word *proskuneo* is translated as "worshipped," but this is really an interpretation and not simply a translation. The scholars who provided these translations interpret(ed) the Canaanite woman's prostration in front of Jesus as an act of worship, but that does not necessarily mean that the woman was worshipping Jesus as one would worship God.

When the magi of Matthew's Gospel locate the infant Jesus they prostrate to him, not because they wanted to worship God, but because they believed that Jesus was "King of the Jews" (Matt. 2:1–12), and as a tribute to the newborn king they presented him with gifts, much like the Queen of Sheba did when she visited King Solomon.[1]

In the book of Revelation the word *proskuneo* relates to an act of prostration that would be extended to members of the Church of Philadelphia by the disbelievers in their community:

> Behold, I will make them of the synagogue of Satan, which say they are Jews, and are not, but do lie; behold, *I will make them to come and worship* (proskuneo) *before thy feet,* and to know that I have loved thee. (Rev. 3:9, KJV)

Certainly John, the author of Revelation, did not mean that these people would be *worshipped* like God, and so neither

---

[1]   See 1 Kings 10:10.

can we assume that Jesus had been "worshipped" by the people who prostrated to him.

Jesus was "worshiped" in the Christian canon, not because he was God, but because he was the "Son of God." In the Gospel according to Matthew, when the disciples see Jesus walking on water, they prostrate themselves to him, saying: "Of a truth thou art the Son of God" (Matt. 14:33, KJV). They do not say, or imply in any way, that they thought Jesus was God. They called him the Son of God because they witnessed firsthand the relationship he had with God. As members of the Jewish community, the disciples were familiar with such paranormal phenomena, as their scriptures are filled with stories of righteous men performing acts of God. They would not, therefore, have been so naïve as to think Jesus was God, even if he did walk on water. Even the narrator of the Gospel realizes that it was the faith of Jesus that allowed him to perform this miracle, a faith that Peter apparently didn't have:

> And he said, Come. And when Peter was come down out of the ship, he walked on the water, to go to Jesus. But when he saw the wind boisterous, he was afraid; and beginning to sink, he cried, saying, Lord, save me. And immediately Jesus stretched forth his hand, and caught him, and said unto him, O thou of little faith, wherefore didst thou doubt? (Matt. 14:29–31, KJV)

Although the disciples, according to both Matthew and Luke, did prostrate themselves to Jesus just prior to his departure, there is no indication in either of these texts that they worshiped him like the "Father." In fact, there is evidence suggesting that they did not worship him. In the Gospel according to Luke, for example, after Jesus is taken up into heaven and the disciples prostrate to him, they return to Jerusalem and *praise* God:

> And he led them out as far as to Bethany, and he lifted up his hands, and blessed them. And it came to pass, while he blessed them, he was parted from them, and carried up into heaven. And *they worshipped* (proskuneo) *him*, and returned to Jerusalem with great joy: And were continually in the temple, *praising and blessing God.* (Luke 24:50–53, KJV)

Similarly, in the book of Acts, when the disciples are ordered by the chief priests and elders to refrain from speaking in the name of Jesus, they offer prayers to God and not Jesus:

> And they called them, and commanded them not to speak at all nor teach in the name of Jesus… And being let go, they went to their own company, and reported all that the chief priests and elders had said unto them. And when they heard that, they lifted up their voice to God with one accord, and said, Lord, thou art God, which hast made heaven, and earth, and the sea, and all that in them is. (Acts 4:18–24, KJV)

God is the one throughout the Christian canon who is worthy of worship. In his first letter to the Corinthians, when Paul describes the reaction of unbelievers to the prophesying of the believers in the church, it is to God they would "fall down" and "worship" (1 Cor. 14:24–25, ASV), not Jesus, and in his letter to the Romans, when Paul embarks on a risky mission to Jerusalem, he urges his followers to pray to God on his behalf, and not to Jesus (Rom. 15:25–32).

In the Gospel according to John, when Jesus discusses the importance of worshipping in Jerusalem with a Samaritan woman, he speaks to her about worshipping the "Father" as though it were common knowledge that *worship*, in the true sense of the word, was to be directed toward the Father (a.k.a. God), and no one else:

> The woman saith unto him, Sir, I perceive that thou art a prophet. Our fathers worshipped in this mountain; and ye say, that in Jerusalem is the place where men ought to worship. Jesus saith unto her, Woman, believe me, the hour cometh, when *ye shall neither in this mountain, nor yet at Jerusalem, worship the Father*. Ye worship ye know not what: we know what we worship: for salvation is of the Jews. But the hour cometh, and now is, when the *true worshippers shall worship the Father* in spirit and in truth: for the Father seeketh such to worship him. God is a Spirit: and they that worship him must worship him in spirit and in truth. (John 4:19–24, KJV)

Even in the apocalypse, where Jesus allegedly speaks to his beloved disciple in a vision, God alone is worthy of worship, and Jesus is merely a prophet who testified to the truth about God:

> And he saith unto me... These are the true
> sayings of God. And I fell at his feet to worship
> him. And he said unto me, See thou do it not:
> I am thy fellowservant, and of thy brethren
> that have the testimony of Jesus: *worship*
> (proskuneo) *God*: for the testimony of Jesus
> is the spirit of prophecy. (Rev. 19:9–10, KJV)

The early evangelists undoubtedly revered Jesus, as did many of the people who encountered him during his brief three-year ministry. They regarded him as the Messiah and heir to the throne of King David, a prophet and a teacher, and a miraculous healer. Thus, it was fitting that, in accordance with the culture and the times in which he lived, Jesus would on occasion be the recipient of an act of prostration. He was not, however, worthy of the worship that is due to God alone, the creator and sustainer of the heavens and the earth. As Jesus says himself, while reportedly being tempted by the devil, "Thou shalt worship the Lord thy God, and him only shalt thou serve" (Luke 4:8, KJV).

CHAPTER 9

Judgment

Among the many similarities between Islam and Christianity is the importance of accountability and belief in a Day of Judgment that will coincide with the resurrection of the dead and the end of the world as we know it. When it comes to the role of Jesus, however, in this inevitable and inescapable trail there is virtually no comparison. In Islam, God alone is the owner of Judgment Day, and Jesus is counted among those who will be judged (along with Muhammad and the thousands of other prophets that preceded him), while in Christianity Jesus is believed to be the one who will judge "the living and the dead" (Acts 10:42, ASV).

The return of Jesus is regarded in Islam as one of the major signs concerning the certainty of the Hour,[1] or Day of Judgment, but is not, as in Christianity, an event that triggers the Day of Judgment. According to the collective *hadith* (words, statements) of Prophet Muhammad there will be many other significant events between the descent of Jesus and the Day of Judgment, and Jesus will have passed away long before then. Prophet Muhammad also indicated that Jesus would establish justice on Earth, but not in the

---

[1]   See chapter 43, verse 61 of the Holy Koran.

form of an "everlasting kingdom." According to *hadith*, Jesus will judge by the law of the Koran.[1]

The Day of Judgment is a topic addressed throughout the Christian canon, although the role of Jesus and the extent to which he would have authority over the judgment process is difficult to decipher. Some evangelists emphasize God's role in the judgment process, while others tend to focus more on Jesus.

In the Gospel according to Matthew the process of judgment is attributed primarily to the Son of Man, as evident from the following passage, where Jesus compares the Son of Man to both a shepherd and a king:

> When the Son of man shall come in his glory, and all the holy angels with him, then shall he sit upon the throne of his glory: And before him shall be gathered all nations: and he shall separate them one from another, as a shepherd divideth his sheep from the goats: And he shall set the sheep on his right hand, but the goats on the left. Then shall the King say unto them on his right hand, Come, ye blessed of my Father, inherit the kingdom prepared for you from the foundation of the world: For I was an hungred, and ye gave me meat: I was thirsty, and ye gave me drink: I was a stranger, and ye took me in: Naked, and ye clothed me: I was sick, and ye visited me: I was in prison, and ye came unto me. Then shall the righteous answer him, saying, Lord, when saw we thee an hungred, and fed

---

[1]   Sahih al-Bukhari, Book of Prophets.

thee? or thirsty, and gave thee drink? When saw we thee a stranger, and took thee in? or naked, and clothed thee? Or when saw we thee sick, or in prison, and came unto thee? And the King shall answer and say unto them, Verily I say unto you, Inasmuch as ye have done it unto one of the least of these my brethren, ye have done it unto me. Then shall he say also unto them on the left hand, Depart from me, ye cursed, into everlasting fire, prepared for the devil and his angels: For I was an hungred, and ye gave me no meat: I was thirsty, and ye gave me no drink: I was a stranger, and ye took me not in: naked, and ye clothed me not: sick, and in prison, and ye visited me not. Then shall they also answer him, saying, Lord, when saw we thee an hungred, or athirst, or a stranger, or naked, or sick, or in prison, and did not minister unto thee? Then shall he answer them, saying, Verily I say unto you, Inasmuch as ye did it not to one of the least of these, ye did it not to me. And these shall go away into everlasting punishment: but the righteous into life eternal. (Matt. 25:31–46, KJV)

Son of Man is an alias assumed by Jesus in all four Gospel narratives, and presumably the same son of man that appears in Daniel's vision of the "four great beasts" and receives dominion and glory from the "Ancient of days," a.k.a. God (Dan. 7:1–14, KJV).[1] The process of judgment in Daniel's dream is attributed solely to the Ancient of days, as the son of man is not even present when "the judgment

---

[1]   For more information on the Son of Man, refer to Chapter 3.

was set, and the books were opened" (Dan. 7:9–10, KJV), and in a subsequent verse it is God, or the Ancient of days, who pronounces judgment in favor of the saints, and not the son of man:

> I beheld, and the same horn made war with the saints, and prevailed against them; *Until the Ancient of days came, and judgment was given* to the saints of the most High; and the time came that the saints possessed the kingdom. (Dan. 7:21–22, KJV)

For Jesus then to say that the Son of Man will come to judge between the nations (Matt. 25:31–46, above) would seem a gross misinterpretation of Daniel's dream, unless we are to assume that God was to delegate the process of judgment in some capacity to his Anointed.

Elsewhere in the Gospel according to Matthew, Jesus reportedly says: "the Son of man shall come *in the glory of his Father*" and "reward every man according to his works" (Matt. 16:27, KJV), perhaps echoing the words of David and Jeremiah concerning the justice they anticipated from the LORD.[1] This time, although Jesus again assumes a role for himself that had traditionally been associated with *Yahweh*, he attributes the glory of this endeavor to the "Father," or, in other words, God. In Acts of the Apostles this point is articulated more clearly when Peter exclaims that Jesus was "ordained of God to be the Judge of the living and the dead" (Acts 10:42, ASV), thereby attributing the process of judgment to Jesus but not the judgment itself.

---

[1]   See Ps. 62:12 and Jer. 17:10.

The idea of Jesus being appointed by God suggests that he would still be in a position of servitude on the Day of Judgment, even though he would supposedly have the authority to judge. Later in the book of Acts Paul reiterates the words of Peter, indicating that God would actually be the one to judge the world, albeit through Jesus, a man "he hath ordained":

> And the times of this ignorance God winked at; but now commandeth all men every where to repent: Because he hath appointed a day, in the which *he will judge* the world in righteousness *by that man whom he hath ordained*; whereof he hath given assurance unto all men, in that he hath raised him from the dead. (Acts 17:30–31, KJV)

In the Gospel according to John, the issue of judgment is given a bit more attention than it is in the synoptics, as the author of the fourth Gospel approaches the subject from a slightly different angle, accentuating the relationship between the pending Day of Judgment and the preaching phase of Jesus's ministry. In chapter three, for example, Jesus allegedly declares: "For God sent not his Son into the world to condemn the world; but that the world through him might be saved. He that believeth on him is not condemned: but he that believeth not is condemned already, because he hath not believed in the name of the only begotten Son of God" (John 3:17–18, KJV). In other words, God sent his anointed "Son" into the world to warn people about the Day of Judgment, and, as a result, some of them would be saved, or "not condemned," while others would be condemned on the Day of Judgment.

In a similar verse Jesus tells the Jews: "He that heareth my word, and believeth on him that sent me, hath everlasting life, and shall not come into condemnation; but is passed from death unto life" (John 5:24, KJV). This time the conditions are different, but the result is the same—the believers would be spared on the Day of Judgment and the disbelievers… well, their fate is addressed in a later passage, where Jesus reiterates his statement from chapter 3, pointing out that the words he spoke would serve as evidence against them on the Day of Judgment:

> And if any man hear my words, and believe not, I judge him not: for I came not to judge the world, but to save the world. He that rejecteth me, and receiveth not my words, hath one that judgeth him: *the word that I have spoken, the same shall judge him in the last day.* (John 12:47–48, KJV)

The words that Jesus spoke, according to John,[1] were actually the words of God, a.k.a. "the Father," and so, from this we can deduce that God is the one who actually judges and not Jesus. In fact, in another Johannine verse, Jesus essentially confirms this when he refers to God as the one who seeks glory for him and judges:

> And I seek not mine own glory: there is one that seeketh and judgeth. Verily, verily, I say unto you, If a man keep my saying, he shall never see death. (John 8:50–51, KJV)

---

[1] See John 12:49–50.

Yes, it is true that Jesus also says in the Gospel according to John that "the Father judgeth no man, but hath committed all judgment unto the Son" (John 5:22, KJV), but in the same passage he attributes the source of this judgment to God:

> *I can of mine own self do nothing: as I hear,*
> *I judge*: and my judgment is just; because I
> seek not mine own will, but the will of the
> Father which hath sent me. (John 5:30, KJV)

After the fall of Babylon in John's book of Revelation, God is praised for his true and just judgments (Rev. 19:1–2), and Jesus is described as a faithful servant who judges in righteousness and makes war (Rev. 19:11). He would tread the winepress of the wrath of God but is not himself divine:

> And out of his mouth goeth a sharp sword,
> that with it he should smite the nations: and
> he shall rule them with a rod of iron: and he
> treadeth the winepress of the fierceness and
> wrath of Almighty God. (Rev. 19:15, KJV)

The reign of Jesus, according to John, is bounded to an undisclosed period of time, which he quantifies as a "thousand years" (Rev. 20:1–6), and when the time finally comes for the judgment to commence, the preeminence of Jesus is overshadowed by the throne of God:

> And *I saw a great white throne, and him that*
> *sat on it, from whose face the earth and the*
> *heaven fled away; and there was found no*
> *place for them.* And I saw the dead, small
> and great, stand before God; and the books

> were opened: and another book was opened, which is the book of life: and the dead were judged out of those things which were written in the books, according to their works. And the sea gave up the dead which were in it; and death and hell delivered up the dead which were in them: and they were judged every man according to their works. And death and hell were cast into the lake of fire… And whosoever was not found written in the book of life was cast into the lake of fire. (Rev. 20:11–15, KJV)

There can be no doubt that the one who sits on the throne in this passage is God, and not Jesus, because only *Yahweh*, the God of Israel, could cause the heavens and the earth to flee from his presence. John's use of this language reflects a firm understanding of the Hebrew Scriptures, where it is said of *Yahweh*, "the heaven and heaven of heavens cannot contain thee" (1 Kings 8:27, KJV). John makes numerous references in his apocalypse to "him that sat" on the throne, and each time it is clear from the context of the passage that God is the one implicated. The first time, for example, that John identifies God in this manner—in chapter 4 of the apocalypse—no mention is made of Jesus until the following chapter, where the Messiah enters the scene as a slain lamb who takes the scroll with the seven seals out of the right hand of "him that sat upon the throne" (Rev. 5:1–7, KJV). In another passage John describes a scene wherein a multitude of people from every nation, tribe, and language appear wearing white robes and proclaiming: "Salvation to our God which sitteth upon the throne, AND[1] unto the Lamb" (Rev. 7:9–10, KJV), while in the same passage the seer is told that, because these people have washed their robes in the blood of the Lamb, they are now "before *the throne of God*" to worship him day and night, and that "*he that sitteth on the throne* shall dwell among them" (Rev. 7:13–15, KJV). "They shall hunger no more," writes John, nor "thirst any more… For the Lamb which is *in the midst of the throne* shall feed them… and God shall wipe away all tears from their eyes" (Rev. 7:16–17, KJV).

The fact that the Lamb is described as being "in the midst of the throne" would seem to suggest that Jesus shared the throne with his "Father" but, in the words of John, in an earlier passage, Jesus was merely given the right to sit on the throne:

> To him that overcometh will I grant to sit with me in my throne, even as I also overcame, and am set down with my Father in *his throne.* (Rev. 3:21, KJV)

In the Gospel according to Matthew, Jesus himself confirms the fact that the throne belongs to God and that it is he (God) who sits upon it:

> And he that shall swear by heaven, sweareth by *the throne of God, and by him that sitteth thereon.* (Matt. 23:22, KJV)

---

[1] Emphasis added.

Paul's evaluation of the Day of Judgment is spelled out clearly in the beginning of his letter to the Romans, which happens to be among the most important letters in the Christian canon in terms of creed and ordinance. Perhaps the most significant feature of this remarkable dissertation is that it is written from a universal perspective to include both Jews and "Greeks."

Paul begins his message to the Romans (after the usual formalities that accompany all of his letters) with a warning about the "wrath of God," which had been "revealed from heaven" against "all ungodliness and unrighteousness of men" (Rom. 1:18, KJV), and then goes on to explain that no one, not even the Gentiles, who knew nothing of the Torah, would be able to plead ignorance on the Day of Judgment, because the evidence of God's existence had been revealed to them in various blessings throughout his creation (Rom. 1:19–20).[1]

After establishing the guilt of the Gentiles, who, as a result of their disbelief, were left by God to perform all types of evil deeds, Paul turns to the Jews and asks: "thinkest thou… that judgest them which do such things, and doest the same, that thou shalt escape *the judgment of God*" (Rom. 2:3, KJV)? The fact that Paul would warn the Jews about "the judgment of God" without so much as mentioning the name of Jesus makes it perfectly clear that he considered God to be the ultimate judge and facilitator of the final judgment. Jesus, according to Mathew, did not even know the day or hour upon which the Day of Judgment was to take place:

---

[1]   See also Acts 14:14–18 and 17:24–28.

> Of that day and hour knoweth no man, no,
> not the angels of heaven, but my Father only.
> (Matt. 24:36, KJV)

As Paul continues his exhortation he refers to a "day of wrath," in which the "righteous judgment of God" would be revealed (Rom. 2:5, KJV), and then outlines the result of this judgment using the same Old Testament passage that Jesus allegedly used of the Son of Man in the Gospel according to Matthew:

> But after thy hardness and impenitent heart
> treasurest up unto thyself wrath against the
> day of wrath and revelation of the righteous
> **judgment of God**; *Who will render to every
> man according to his deeds*: (Rom. 2:5–
> 6, KJV)

> For the Son of man shall come in the glory of
> his Father with his angels; and then he shall
> reward every man according to his works.
> (Matt. 16:27, KJV)

> Also unto thee, O Lord, belongeth mercy: for
> thou renderest to every man according to his
> work. (Ps. 62:12, KJV)

The "day of wrath" is an expression made synonymous with the "day of the LORD" in Hebrew scripture[1] and both expressions refer to a dreadful day of judgment that would be unleashed on the world by *Yahweh*, the God of Israel, and not the Messiah. As a member of the Jewish community, Paul undoubtedly understood the significance of the "day

---

[1] See Zeph. 1:14–16.

of the LORD" and, thus, warned his people, as did the prophets of the Old Testament, but, like Matthew and others whose written testimony has found its way into the Christian canon, believed that Jesus would have a role in this final judgment, and so, after explaining how the Jews and the Gentiles would be judged in a similar manner (Rom. 2:12–15), Paul declares that all of this would take place "in the day when *God shall judge* the secrets of men, according to my good news, ***through*** *Jesus Christ*" (Rom. 2:16, YLT).

Paul's summary of the judgment process encapsulates the view of the Judeo-Christian community that revered Jesus within the boundaries of the Hebrew Bible, wherein God is the ultimate judge, and the Messiah his servant. The early evangelists understandably attributed some form of judgment to Jesus as the heir to David's throne but never in the same capacity as God. Even in cases where Jesus is associated with the final judgment, his role is clearly distinguished from that of the "Father." Unfortunately, through the deification of Christ by later generations, those distinctions that were drawn by the early evangelists between God and Jesus have become distorted and subdued to the point where anything that belongs to God belongs to Jesus.

CHAPTER 10

The Holy Spirit

As mentioned earlier, in the chapter entitled "Son of God," Trinity is a word that appears nowhere in the Christian canon, and so it would seem that the early evangelists who provided this testimony knew nothing about the God of "orthodox" Christianity that supposedly exists as one deity in three persons. The authors of the New Testament spoke frequently of the Father, Son, and Holy Spirit, but rarely did they mention all three members of the "Blessed Trinity" together at the same time, and the only one that they ever refer to as God is the "Father." To put it into perspective, there are thirteen verses in the King James Version of the Bible in which the phrase "God the Father" appears and no verses that equate the Son or the Holy Spirit with God.

In both the Hebrew Bible and the Christian canon, God is described metaphorically as the "Father" of the Israelites[1] while the Son and Holy Spirit are connected only through association with the Almighty. Jesus, for example, is identified as the *Son* "of God" (Heb. 4:14, KJV) who would assume the throne of David in accordance with the scriptures,[2] while the Holy Spirit is portrayed as an entity,

---

[1]   See Deut. 32:6, John 8:41–42.

[2]   See Heb. 1:5, 2 Sam. 7:14, and Ps. 2:7.

or attribute, that God would transpose, or instill into the hearts of men:

> If ye then, being evil, know how to give good gifts unto your children: how much more shall your heavenly Father give the Holy Spirit to them that ask him? (Luke 11:13, KJV)

> Then he remembered the days of old, Moses, and his people, saying, Where is he that brought them up out of the sea with the shepherd of his flock? where is he that put his holy Spirit within him? (Isa. 63:11, KJV)

It stands to reason then that the Holy Spirit, like Jesus, is not an integral part of the deity that the early evangelists referred to as Lord, God, and Father, but rather, an expression that was used in biblical times to characterize the power, or "presence" of God.

In the infancy narratives of Luke and Matthew, the Holy Spirit is said to have "come upon" the Virgin Mary and facilitated the conception of Jesus.[1] To think that God himself was present during this remarkable and implausible event when, according to Jewish scripture, "the heaven and heaven of heavens" (1 Kings 8:27, KJV) could not contain the Almighty, is unfathomable. The authors of these enigmatic narrations undoubtedly understood the greatness of God in relation to his creation, as much of their testimony is based on these ancient Hebrew texts. They could not, therefore, have been thinking of the Holy Spirit as God, or some other mode of existence equal to the "Father," when they

---

[1] See Matt. 1:18 and Luke 1:35.

wrote about the miraculous conception of Jesus through the Holy Spirit. Perhaps, more likely, they were referring to the metaphysical force behind this otherwise unexplainable event as the Holy Spirit in the same way that the authors of the Old Testament used the expression "Spirit of the LORD" in reference to similar occurrences. In the second book of Kings, for instance, when the "sons of the prophets" from Jericho see Elijah taken up to heaven in a whirlwind, they say to Elisha, his understudy, "Behold now, there be with thy servants fifty strong men; let them go, we pray thee, and seek thy master: lest peradventure *the Spirit of the LORD hath taken him* up, and cast him upon some mountain, or into some valley" (2 Kings 2:11–16, KJV).

The expression "Spirit of the LORD," in all its various forms and innuendos, is used throughout the Hebrew scripture in a variety of different contexts and appears to be a catch-all phrase for anything of, or relating to, the "presence" of God or the "hand" of God. In the book of Judges, for example, the "Spirit of the LORD" enables Samson to tear a lion to pieces (Judg. 14:5–6), while in the prophetic book of Samuel the "Spirit of the LORD" speaks through the mouth of David:

> Now these be the last words of David... The
> Spirit of the LORD spake by me, and his word
> was in my tongue. (2 Sam. 23:1–2, KJV)

In Luke's Acts of the Apostles the same "Spirit of the LORD" that spoke through David is referred to by Peter as the Holy Spirit,[1] and so it would appear from this that the

---

[1]   See Acts 1:15–16.

two expressions, "Holy Spirit" and "Spirit of the LORD," were used interchangeably in Judeo-Christian tradition.

Perhaps the most important function or manifestation of the Holy Spirit in the Old Testament is the widely prophesized event known as the pouring out of God's Spirit onto the children of Israel during messianic times, described in the following verse from the book of Isaiah:[1]

> Yet now hear, O Jacob my servant; and Israel, whom I have chosen: Thus saith the LORD that made thee, and formed thee from the womb, which will help thee… For I will pour water upon him that is thirsty, and floods upon the dry ground: *I will pour my spirit upon thy seed,* and my blessing upon thine offspring: (Isa. 44:1–3, KJV)

In the New Testament, fulfillment of these prophecies begins with the descent of the Holy Spirit onto Jesus at the beginning of his ministry in the form of a dove—an event recorded in all four Gospel narratives, although Luke is the only evangelist who refers to the spirit from above as holy:

> Now it came to pass, when all the people were baptized, that, Jesus also having been baptized, and praying, the heaven was opened, and *the Holy Spirit descended in a bodily form, as a dove,* upon him, and a voice came out of heaven, Thou art my beloved Son; in thee I am well pleased. (Luke 3:21–22, ASV)

---

[1] See also Isa. 32:15, Ezek. 37:13–14, and Joel 3:1–2 (2:28–32 in Protestant versions).

According to Matthew, it is the "Spirit of God" (Matt. 3:16) that descends onto Jesus, while in both Mark and John's account it is simply "the Spirit" that descends (Mark 1:10, John 1:32).

In all four Gospel narratives Jesus is declared to be the Son of God after the spirit descends, in what would seem to be an official anointing, making him the Messiah of the Lord:

> And Jesus, when he was baptized, went up straightway out of the water: and, lo, the heavens were opened unto him, and he saw the Spirit of God descending like a dove, and lighting upon him: And lo a voice from heaven,[1] saying, This is my beloved Son, in whom I am well pleased. (Matt. 3:16–17, KJV)

Filled with the Holy Spirit, Jesus was now prepared to speak the word of God and deliver the gospel to his people in much the same way that other leaders and prophets of the Old Testament were prepared for their missions when the "Spirit of the LORD" came upon them.[2]

This, of course, begs the question: if Jesus were indeed "true God and true man" what would have been the purpose of having the Holy Spirit descend upon him? Wouldn't he have already had the Spirit of God in him?

---

[1]   In the fourth Gospel (John 1:34) John the Baptist is the one who declares Jesus to be the Son of God in lieu of the "voice form heaven"; see also Mark 1:11 and Luke 3:22.

[2]   See Judg. 3:7–11, 1 Sam. 10:1–7, Ezek. 11:1–13.

The fact of the matter is that nowhere in the Christian canon is Jesus portrayed (explicitly) as God. Even as the "Son of God" he still needed to receive the "Spirit of God" like any other servant appointed by the Almighty, and this undoubtedly is the explanation of the fact that in the Gospel according to Matthew, Jesus is identified as the chosen servant in the book of Isaiah upon whom God would place his Spirit,[1] or why, in the Gospel according to Luke, Jesus identifies himself as a prophet, empowered by the Spirit of the Lord, after quoting another passage from the scroll of Isaiah:

> And Jesus returned *in the power of the Spirit* into Galilee: and there went out a fame of him through all the region round about... And he came to Nazareth, where he had been brought up: and, as his custom was, he went into the synagogue on the sabbath day, and stood up for to read. And there was delivered unto him the book of the prophet Esaias. And when he had opened the book, he found the place where it was written, *The Spirit of the Lord is upon me, because he hath anointed me* to preach the gospel to the poor; he hath sent me to... preach deliverance to the captives, and recovering of sight to the blind, to set at liberty them that are bruised, To preach the acceptable year of the Lord. And he closed the book, and he gave it again to the minister, and sat down. And the eyes of all them that were in the synagogue were fastened on him. And he began to say unto them, This day is this scripture fulfilled in your

---

[1] See Matt. 12:17–18.

> ears. And all bare him witness, and wondered
> at the gracious words which proceeded out of
> his mouth. And they said, Is not this Joseph's
> son? And he said, Verily I say unto you, *No
> prophet is accepted in his own country.* (Luke
> 4:14–24, KJV)

The descent of the Holy Spirit onto the body of Jesus is preceded in the gospel narratives by an announcement from John the Baptist about how his baptism of water would be replaced by Jesus, who would baptize with the Holy Spirit:

> And John was clothed with camel's hair,
> and with a girdle of a skin about his loins;
> and he did eat locusts and wild honey; And
> preached, saying, There cometh one mightier
> than I after me, the latchet of whose shoes I
> am not worthy to stoop down and unloose. *I
> indeed have baptized you with water: but he
> shall baptize you with the Holy Ghost.*[1] (Mark
> 1:6–8, KJV)

In the Gospel according to Luke, as well as the Matthean parallel, the baptism of Jesus is expanded to include a baptism of fire,[2] which would seem to be a prophecy pertaining to the *Parousia,* or second "coming" of Christ, and one that Jesus would not be equipped to fulfill during the "Passion" phase of his ministry. Thus, we read in Luke's second letter to Theophilus[3] that, at the time of the Ascension, the only

---

[1] See also Matt. 3:11–12, Luke 3:15–17, and John 1:32–33.

[2] Luke 3:16, Matt. 3:11.

[3] Both the Gospel according to Luke and Acts of the Apostles are addressed to an unknown ruler named Theophilus.

baptism the disciples were to receive is that of the Holy Spirit:

> For John truly baptized with water; but ye shall be baptized with the Holy Ghost not many days hence. (Acts 1:5, KJV)

The disciples apparently interpret this as the pouring out of God's spirit that had been prophesized in their scripture and, in anticipation of the fulfillment of these prophecies, ask their master: "Lord, wilt thou at this time restore again the kingdom to Israel" (Acts 1:6, KJV)?

Knowing that he would not be able to give them the temporal power they desired, Jesus explains to his disciples that they would have to continue waiting for the full realization of these messianic prophecies but would receive "power" through the Holy Spirit that would enable them to be witnesses to all the prophecies that had been fulfilled thus far:

> And he said unto them, It is not for you to know the times or the seasons, which the Father hath put in his own power. But *ye shall receive power, after that the Holy Ghost is come upon you*: and ye shall be witnesses unto me both in Jerusalem, and in all Judaea, and in Samaria, and unto the uttermost part of the earth. (Acts 1:7–8, KJV)

The manner in which the Holy Spirit would be transmitted from Jesus to his followers is not clearly explained in the Christian canon, or at least not in a consistent fashion. The generally accepted story is the one that Luke relates in Acts of the Apostles, where, shortly after the Ascension of Jesus, the Holy Spirit descends in the form of fiery tongues that come to rest on each of the disciples:

> And when the day of Pentecost was fully come, they were all with one accord in one place. And suddenly there came a sound from heaven as of a rushing mighty wind, and it filled all the house where they were sitting. And there appeared unto them cloven tongues like as of fire, and it sat upon each of them. And they were all filled with the Holy Ghost, and began to speak with other tongues, as the Spirit gave them utterance. (Acts 2:1–4, KJV)

This bizarre tale is exclusive to Luke, who further relates that, as the disciples began to preach the gospel in the various languages of those who were visiting Jerusalem from neighboring regions, the people were amazed and could offer only as an explanation that they must have been drunk (Acts 2:5–13). In response to this Peter stands up and proclaims to the crowd that what they were witnessing was the fulfillment of a prophecy announced long ago by Joel pertaining to the pouring out of God's spirit "upon all flesh" in messianic times:

> And it shall come to pass in the last days, saith God, *I will pour out of my Spirit upon all flesh*: and your sons and your daughters shall prophesy, and your young men shall see visions, and your old men shall dream dreams: And on my servants and on my handmaidens I will pour out in those days

of my Spirit; and they shall prophesy. (Acts 2:17–18, KJV)

As Peter continues to preach to the crowd about the fulfillment of prophecy, he emphasizes that Jesus was first to receive the promise of the Holy Spirit from God and that he in turn had "poured forth" the spirit that he received onto his disciples:

> This Jesus did God raise up, whereof we all are witnesses. Being therefore by the right hand of God exalted, and *having received of the Father the promise of the Holy Spirit, he hath poured forth this, which ye see and hear.* (Acts 2:32–33, ASV)

Convinced by the arguments that Peter allegedly brought forth, the crowd eventually asks: "brethren, what shall we do" (Acts 2:37, KJV)?

In response to this newfound enthusiasm the disciple, upon whom Jesus reportedly intended to build his church,[1] instructs the crowd to "repent" and "be baptized" so that they would receive the "gift of the Holy Spirit" (Acts 2:38, ASV). This formula, however, for receiving the Holy Spirit is deemed inadequate by Luke later in the narration:

> Now when the apostles which were at Jerusalem heard that Samaria had received the word of God, they sent unto them Peter and John: Who, when they were come down, prayed for them, that they might receive the

---

[1]   See Matt. 16:17–19.

> Holy Ghost: (For as yet he was fallen upon
> none of them: only they were baptized in the
> name of the Lord Jesus.) Then laid they their
> hands on them, and they received the Holy
> Ghost. (Acts 8:14–17, KJV)

To complicate things further, Luke infers in another verse that it was possible to receive the Holy Spirit without being baptized:

> While Peter yet spake these words, the Holy
> Ghost fell on all them which heard the word.
> And they of the circumcision which believed
> were astonished, as many as came with Peter,
> because that on the Gentiles also was poured
> out the gift of the Holy Ghost. For they heard
> them speak with tongues, and magnify God.
> Then answered Peter, Can any man forbid
> water, that these should not be baptized,
> which have received the Holy Ghost as
> well as we? And he commanded them to
> be baptized in the name of the Lord. (Acts
> 10:44–48, KJV)

The only logical conclusion, it seems, that one could draw from all this is that Luke didn't know exactly how the Holy Spirit was expected to be poured out. He undoubtedly believed that Jesus was the Messiah and wanted others to believe but, like many of the early evangelists, relied upon oral traditions that weren't always sound. His exclusive account of the Holy Spirit and how it affected the early Christian community would perhaps be more credible if only there was something to compare it to, but as it stands Luke's Acts of the Apostles is the only book in the Bible that deals with the post-Ascension activities of the twelve disciples.

In his various letters to the surrounding Gentile communities, Paul uses language similar to that of Luke and, like his companion (in the latter half of Acts), fails to give a clear and consistent account of how the Holy Spirit was supposed to have been poured forth on "all flesh" in accordance with Joel's prophecy (Joel 2:28). In one verse Paul indicates that it would be through faith that one would receive "the promise of the Spirit" (Gal. 3:14, KJV), while in another verse he proclaims: "by one Spirit are we all baptized into one body," after explaining how different members of the church would receive different "gifts," or talents, from the same "Spirit" (1 Cor. 12:1–13, KJV).

In the same passage Paul notes that, in addition to the diversity of gifts coming from the same Spirit, there would be "differences of administrations, but the same Lord (Jesus)" and "diversities of operations" but the same God "which worketh all in all" (1 Cor. 12:4–6, KJV). The same distinction the evangelist makes between God, the Father, and Jesus, the Lord at the beginning of this and every letter he wrote, is applied here to differentiate between the "same God," the "same Spirit" and the "same Lord" (Jesus); and so we see that, although Paul clearly identifies all three members of the Christian trinity, he refers only to one as God.

Out of all the remaining apostolic traditions the Johannine branch is the only one that mentions anything about the gift of the Holy Spirit or how it would be transferred from

Jesus to his followers. The importance of baptism is outlined at the end of Mark's Gospel, but no mention is made of the Holy Spirit or fulfillment of prophecy:

> He that believeth and is baptized shall be saved; but he that believeth not shall be damned. (Mark 16:16, KJV)

At the end of Matthew, Jesus instructs his disciples to baptize in the name of the Father, Son, and Holy Spirit, but gives no indication as to whether or not this would enable them to receive the gift of the Holy Spirit or transfer it to others:

> Go ye therefore, and teach all nations, baptizing them in the name of the Father, and of the Son, and of the Holy Ghost. (Matt. 28:19, KJV)

John, on the other hand, indicates clearly in the Gospel which bears his name that those who believed in Jesus would receive "the Spirit."[1] John does not, however, mention anything about tongues of fire, baptism, or the laying of hands as a means through which believers could receive the Holy Spirit. Instead, he describes an event at the end of his Gospel in which Jesus simply breathes the gift of the Holy Spirit onto his disciples:

> Then the same day at evening, being the first day of the week, when the doors were shut where the disciples were assembled for fear of the Jews, came Jesus and stood in the midst, and saith unto them, Peace be unto

---

[1] See John 7:37–39.

> you. And when he had so said, he shewed
> unto them his hands and his side. Then were
> the disciples glad, when they saw the LORD.
> Then said Jesus to them again, Peace be unto
> you: as my Father hath sent me, even so send
> I you. And when he had said this, *he breathed*
> *on them, and saith unto them, Receive ye the*
> *Holy Ghost.* (John 20:19–22, KJV)

The stark reality behind all of these irreconcilable differences regarding the gift of the Holy Spirit that must be acknowledged is that no one within the early Christian community had any definite knowledge about the Holy Spirit. The term was obviously derived from the Hebrew Bible, where the "Spirit of the Lord" is applied to practically anything associated with God, but nowhere in the Christian canon is the exact nature of this abstract *spiritual* entity defined in clear terms. About the only thing that the early evangelists do agree on is that the Holy Spirit is not God, and certainly not Jesus.

CHAPTER 11

In the Name of Jesus

If there's one idiosyncrasy associated with the Bible that stands in contrast with the spirit of Islam it would be the numerous references to various acts of faith and invocations that are said to have been done in the name of Jesus; most notably, in the fourth Gospel, where the prophet says to his disciples: "whatsoever ye shall ask of the Father *in my name*, he may give it you" (John 15:16, KJV). In Islam it is unthinkable to invoke the name of anyone other than Allah (God), but to the authors of the New Testament it was presumably acceptable to call upon the name of Jesus when seeking the help of God, and this undoubtedly has abetted the immoderate admiration of Jesus, which eventually led to the deification of Christ. But does this necessarily mean that the early evangelists believed that Jesus was God?

We learn from the book of Acts that, after he was taken up into heaven, the disciples of Jesus began to perform miracles[1] while proclaiming his name (although the Koran does not confirm this) and, as they did, many people came to believe; and, incidentally, in the Gospel according to John, during the final gathering of Jesus with his disciples before the arrest, this is precisely what their master instructs them to do.

---

[1]   Acts 3:6, Acts 8:7, Acts 9:33–34, Acts 9:36–42, and Acts 14:3.

In John's version of the Last Supper, Jesus reportedly meets with his disciples around an evening meal to inform them that he would be leaving them soon and that, although they could not join him on his journey, they would eventually follow him (John 13:33–36).

The disciples apparently had a difficult time comprehending this and asked questions like, "Lord, why cannot I follow thee now?" (John 13:37, KJV), or, "Lord, we know not whither thou goest; and how can we know the way" (John 14:5, KJV)?

In response to Philip, who asks, "Lord, show us the Father, and it sufficeth us" (John 14:8, KJV), Jesus explains that the Father was *in*[1] him and that if they could not believe it when he told them they should at least believe on the merit of the miracles he performed in front of them, as these would serve to substantiate his claim (John 14:10–11).

Then, after clarifying his relationship with "the Father," Jesus takes the discussion a step further and says: "verily, I say unto you, He that believeth on me," meaning that the Father was *in* him, "the works that I do shall he do also; and greater works than these shall he do; because I go unto my Father. And whatsoever ye shall ask in my name, that will I do, *that the Father may be glorified in the Son*" (John 14:12–13, KJV). In other words, the disciples who believed that Jesus was the Messiah were to continue on after his departure with the work that he was doing, including the miracles; and these miracles, according to John, were to be

---

[1] See Chapter 4 for further discussion on this passage.

done in the name of Jesus so that "the Father may be glorified in the Son." Although the evangelist does portray Jesus as having the power to orchestrate miracles, he attributes the glory of these miracles to God (a.k.a. the Father).

The mission of the disciples to be apostles on behalf of their "lord" is reiterated several times by Jesus in his final meeting with them, and each time it is the glory of the "Father" that reigns paramount. On two occasions Jesus tells his disciples: "Whatsoever ye shall ask the Father in my name, *he will give it* you,"[1] indicating that God is the one who actually provides for his servants and that Jesus is but a middleman or intercessor.

This paradigm is manifested throughout the Gospel narratives in a variety of ways and different aspects of Jesus's ministry. In the synoptic Gospels, for example, when Jesus sees his disciples arguing over whom amongst them was the most righteous, the prophet explains: "Whosoever shall receive one of such children *in my name*, receiveth me: and whosoever shall receive me, receiveth not me, but him that sent me" (Mark 9:37, KJV).[2] The one who sent Jesus, of course, is God, and so, by welcoming the little children in the name of Jesus, the disciples are taught, they would actually be welcoming him (God, that is).

The disciples are encouraged in the Christian canon to do virtually everything in the name of Jesus; not out of respect for his alleged divinity, but because of the association he had

---

[1]   John 16:23 (see also John 15:16).

[2]   See also Matt. 18:5 and Luke 9:48.

with God. Take, for example, Paul's advice to the Colossians, where the evangelist urges his community: "whatsoever ye do, in word or in deed, do all in the name of the Lord Jesus, *giving thanks to God* the Father **through** him" (Col. 3:17, ASV). The ultimate goal in all of these acts was to praise God, but the preeminence of Jesus in the hearts and minds of the early evangelists was too great to suppress, and so it was deemed fitting to invoke his name alongside the one who anointed him and sent him into the world. Jesus is the one, according to all four Gospel narratives, who was to come "*in the name* of the Lord (*Yahweh*),"[1] which made him a representative of the "Father," or in other words, a prophet; and to the authors of the New Testament this was a two-way street, wherein the ordinary believers could communicate to God through Jesus, just as God would communicate to them through his prophet.

Miracles were allegedly performed in the name of Jesus, but the disciples, according to Luke, understood that God was the real power behind these events. In his second book, Acts of the Apostles, Luke describes a scene wherein the young community of believers that formed after Jesus had reportedly ascended into heaven seeks the help of God to stretch out his hand and perform miraculous signs in the name of Jesus:

> And being let go, they came to their own company, and reported all that the chief priests and the elders had said unto them. And they, when they heard it, *lifted up their voice to God* with one accord, and said, O

---

[1]   Matt 21:9, Mark 11:9, Luke 19:38, John 12:13.

> Lord, thou that didst make the heaven and the earth and the sea, and all that in them is… And now, Lord, look upon their threatenings: and grant unto thy servants to speak thy word with all boldness, while thy *stretchest forth thy hand to heal; and that signs and wonders may be done* **through the name** *of thy holy Servant Jesus.* (Acts 4:23–30, ASV)

The disciples held the honorable distinction of being apostles of Jesus, who referred to himself repeatedly as God's apostle.[1] Hence, it was important for them to preach "in the name of Jesus," and what they preached, according to Luke, was "repentance and remission of sins" (Luke 24:47, KJV); the same message that John the Baptist allegedly preached:

> Now in the fifteenth year of the reign of Tiberius Caesar… the word of God came unto John the son of Zacharias in the wilderness. And he came into all the country about Jordan, *preaching the baptism of repentance for the remission of sins.* (Luke 3:1–3, KJV)

Naturally this meant that the baptism of John would now be done in the name of Jesus, although Matthew adds the "Father" and his Holy Spirit to the equation:

> Then Peter said unto them, Repent, and be baptized every one of you in the name of Jesus Christ for the remission of sins. (Acts 2:38, KJV)

---

[1]   Matt. 10:40, Mark 9:37, Luke 10:16, and John 12:44.

> Go ye therefore, and teach all nations,
> baptizing them in the name of the Father,
> and of the Son, and of the Holy Ghost. (Matt.
> 28:19, KJV)

In some portions of the Bible, extreme preponderance is placed on the name of Jesus to the point of exaltation, although at no time in any of these passages is Jesus confused with God. In his letter to the Philippians, for example, Paul writes that, as a result of his humbleness and obedience, Jesus was exalted by God, who had "given him *a name which is above every name*: That at the name of Jesus every knee should bow... And that every tongue should confess that Jesus Christ is Lord, **to the glory of God the Father**" (Phil. 2:9–11, KJV).

Of course, the only way that God could exalt Jesus is if they were two distinct beings, and, although Paul would have every knee bow and every tongue confess that Jesus is Lord, it is to the glory of God, he stresses, that this should be done.

When Paul says that the name of Jesus is above every name, it's hard to imagine that this would include God's name because, for one thing, the name Jesus (*Yehoshua* in Hebrew) is derived from *Yahweh,* the name given to God in the Torah, and, secondly, this would defy the very spirit of the Hebrew Bible and the faith to which Paul presumably adhered.

Similarly, in the book of Acts, when Peter says to the chief priests and teachers of the law: "in none other is there salvation" (Acts 4:12, ASV)—meaning Jesus, he undoubtedly excludes *Yahweh*, the savior of the Old Testament, from this equation, for if he hadn't his interrogators would surely have accused him of blasphemy, and, moreover, Peter specifies in the very same verse that it was only those names given to men that the disciple was referring to, and thus, only human deliverers:

> Neither is there salvation in any other: for there is none other name under heaven *given among men*, whereby we must be saved. (Acts 4:12, KJV)

According to the author of Hebrews, who may or may not have been Paul, Jesus had become superior to, or "much better" than, the angels, "as he hath by inheritance obtained a more excellent name than they" (Heb. 1:4, KJV). This, of course, begs the question: what name did Jesus inherit, but, more importantly, it provides a glimpse inside the mind of the author and a better understanding of what the early evangelists believed of Jesus. The fact that Jesus is compared in the verse to angels and not God alludes to a barrier that existed in Judeo-Christian tradition between God and man in terms of supremacy and essence, a barrier that the author of Hebrews was apparently not willing to cross.

To say that Jesus was superior to angels is certainly a tremendous commendation, but in no way does this make him divine; in fact, this statement is consistent with the Islamic view of Jesus.

In the second *Surah,* or chapter, of the Koran, when Allah (God) informs the angels about his plan to place man as a vicegerent on earth, they respond: "Wilt thou place therein one who will make mischief and shed blood whilst we do celebrate thy praises and glorify thy holy name" (Al-Baqarah:30)? Having served their Lord for eons with unflinching obedience, the angels question man's ability to live peacefully in accordance with the will of Allah. In the same verse Allah replies: "I know what ye know not," and then, after teaching Adam the "names of all things," asks the angels: "Tell me the names of these if you are truthful" (Al-Baqarah:31). When the angels realize that—with their limited knowledge, they are not necessarily superior to man, Allah commands them to prostrate before Adam (Al-Baqarah:32–34). From this scholars deduce that, because of his free will, man has the capability of exceeding the angels in righteousness because, unlike the angels, man must overcome his desires to obey Allah, whereas the angels are preprogrammed, or created, to obey Allah,[1] and Jesus, as the Messiah and prophet of Allah, was certainly among those who exceeded the angels in this regard.

As for the name that Jesus "inherited," there is nothing special or unique about it. It is the same name given to the successor to Moses, known to English-speaking students as *Joshua*, and God knows how many other Israelites. Joshua (Hebrew, *Yehoshua*) does contain the sacred name for God (*Yahweh*) in Jewish tradition, but the same can be said for many other Hebrew names.

It is certainly possible that the author of Hebrews was referring to some other name when he said that Jesus "hath

---

[1]   According to Islamic tradition angels are without free will and incapable of disobeying Allah.

by inheritance obtained a more excellent name" than the angels (Heb. 1:4, above), but there's nothing in the text to suggest what that name might be. The only other name given to Jesus in the Christian canon that isn't, in reality, a title or an attribute is Immanuel, but this name was known only to Matthew.

In the book of Revelation, Jesus refers to a new name that would be given to him at some point in the future but, at the same time, makes it clear that he and his God had different names:

> Him that overcometh will I make a pillar in the temple of my God, and he shall go no more out: and I will write upon him *the name of **my God***, and the name of the city of my God, which is new Jerusalem, which cometh down out of heaven from my God: and I will write upon him *my new name*. (Rev. 3:12, KJV)

Unfortunately, John does not elaborate much on what this "new name" for Jesus was supposed to be, although he does present in a subsequent passage a cluster of names that presumably belong to Jesus and could certainly qualify as new.

At the end of his apocalypse, as the events leading up to the final judgment unfold, John describes an amazing scene wherein the heavens are opened and there to behold is an extraordinary man riding a white horse, who we're told is "called Faithful and True" (Rev. 19:11, KJV) and who few would argue is an eschatological representation of Jesus.[1] Among the many details the seer notices about the man is that "on his head were many crowns" and that he had a name written on him "that no man knew, but he himself" (Rev. 19:12, KJV). The next thing John relates is that the rider of the horse was "clothed with a vesture dipped in blood" and that "his name is called The Word of God" (Rev. 19:13, KJV). To this point, then, we have two names identified for the rider—"Faithful and True" and "Word of God"—and a third that was known only to him. But John does not stop there. After describing the "armies which were in heaven" (Rev. 19:14, KJV) and a sword coming out of the mouth of the rider, he notes that the mysterious warrior has "on his vesture and on his thigh a name written, KING OF KINGS, AND LORD OF LORDS" (Rev. 19:16, KJV).

"Faithful and True" is a name that exemplifies Jesus's obedience to God and, as such, can only be regarded as an affirmation of his humanity.

The name "Word of God" is undoubtedly connected to the Logos of the fourth Gospel, about which we have already discussed at length. The appellation, as it is used here, however, lacks the element of personification that characterizes the gospel passage and would seem to be analogous with the name "Son of God," as the two expressions are grammatically identical in the Greek.

"King of kings" is an expression used exclusively of human rulers in the Old Testament, while "Lord of lords" is reserved

---

[1]   See Rev. 19:11–21.

for God. In the New Testament, Paul, or perhaps one of his students, applies both titles to God,[1] but in the book of Revelation Jesus is "King of kings" and "Lord of lords."[2] In Chapter 2 we learned that every king is lord and that the Messiah is both lord and king, so it's not surprising to see one of the early evangelists refer to Jesus in this manner; especially if we consider the fact that Christ was expected to rule Israel in the messianic age, a time when Jerusalem would become the city through which God would establish his everlasting kingdom. As the Messiah of this new and coming age, Jesus was thus set apart from all other Israelite kings, but still human, and according to both John and Paul only slated to rule for a period time.[3]

The early evangelists referred to Jesus through many names and titles in the Christian canon, but at no time did they ever refer to him as God. They reportedly preached salvation in the name of Jesus and performed miracles in his name, but the intention behind all of this, as we have seen, was to gain access to the "Father" and bring glory to his name. It is God, the Father whom they sought, and God, the Father that Jesus offered them when he reportedly said: "no man cometh unto the Father, but by[4] me" (John 14:6, KJV).

---

[1]   See 1 Tim. 6:13–16.

[2]   See also Rev. 17:14.

[3]   Rev. 20 and 1 Cor. 15:12–28.

[4]   In some translations: "through me."

CHAPTER 12

The Transfiguration

Among the many narratives common to Matthew, Mark, and Luke, none are perhaps as sensational and widely misunderstood as the Transfiguration of Jesus. Cleverly devised to convince Jewish readers that Jesus is the Messiah, it is seldom seen as anything other than a revelation of his divinity, despite the fact that the entire story seems fabricated and that there is little or no evidence to suggest that the incident was intended to portray Jesus as God.

In all three versions of the Transfiguration, the disciples that were with Jesus see Moses and Elijah appear out of nowhere, become afraid, and then notice that the men are gone.[1] No explanation is given, however, in either version, as to how these disciples were able to recognize two prophets from the distant past they had never seen before, or why these prophets appeared. The story seems to have been constructed as an illustration of how Jesus fulfilled both the "law" (represented by Moses) and "the prophets" (represented by Elijah).

The appearance of Elijah and the ensuing conversation regarding his coming[2] was undoubtedly intended to show

---

[1]   Matt. 17:3–4, Mark 9:4–5, Luke 9:30–33.

[2]   Matt. 17:10–13, Mark 9:11–13.

that, in accordance with Malachi 3:23 of the Masoretic text, the messianic age had indeed arrived, and Jesus, therefore, must be the Messiah. In order for the evangelists to have any success, however, in recruiting the Jews, they would need to convince them that Jesus was on par with Moses, their former deliverer, and this, most likely, is the reason for his appearance during the Transfiguration. Both the setting on the mountain and the cloud that "overshadowed them"[1] bear a striking resemblance to the scene in Exodus 24 where Moses goes up Mount Sinai to receive the law.

As far as the actual Transfiguration is concerned, little is said in the biblical text except that the clothing of Jesus became white and that the appearance of his face had changed. In the words of Matthew, "his face did shine as the sun, and his raiment was *white as the light*" (Matt. 17:2, KJV), while in Luke's account, "the fashion of his countenance was altered, and his raiment was *white and glistering*" (Luke 9:29, KJV). In Mark's version, nothing is said about the face of Jesus; however, the evangelist does concur that the garments of Jesus became "glistering, *exceeding white*" (Mark 9:3, ASV).

The appearance of Jesus in bright white clothing is likened by Christian scholars to the appearance of the "Ancient of days" wearing a garment "white as snow" in Daniel's first apocalyptic vision (Dan. 7:9, KJV). "Ancient of days" is an appellation that points unmistakably to God; however, the problem with this supposition is that (1) none of the

---

[1]   Matt. 17:5, Mark 9:7, Luke 9:34–35.

evangelists use the word "snow"[1] in their description of Jesus on the mountain with his disciples, (2) nothing is said about the face of the Ancient of days in Daniel's vision, and (3) there is no real significance to having the robe of Jesus transform because that would not have been part of his being.

It would seem reasonable—in order to accept any connection between the Transfiguration of Jesus and the Ancient of days in Daniel's vision—that we should expect to see the word *snow* in at least one of the three accounts of the Transfiguration, or else some sort of reference to the face of the Ancient of days in the Old Testament passage. Moreover, if the purpose of the Transfiguration was to reveal the divine nature of Jesus, why is there no explanation to this effect in any of the narrations? All that is said is that Jesus is the Son of God, which is nothing more than an emphatic way of calling him the Messiah. Furthermore, it would make no sense to have Jesus reveal his divinity to only three of his disciples, especially when it is explicitly stated in the Gospel according to John: "No man hath seen God at any time" (John 1:18, KJV).

Indeed it is no accident that Daniel avoids making reference to the countenance of God in his vision. As a devout Jew dedicated to the law,[2] Daniel would undoubtedly have been familiar with the story of Moses; who, after asking his Lord,

---

[1]   In some versions of the Bible the word "snow" appears in Mark 9:3; however, most of the Greek texts omit this term.

[2]   See Dan. 1:8–17.

"Show me… thy glory," is told: "Thou canst not see my face; for man shall not see me and live" (Exod. 33:18–20, ASV).

Presumably the authors of the synoptic Gospels were equally familiar with the Hebrew scriptures and did not intend to connect Jesus with the Ancient of days. It does seem plausible, however, that the Transfiguration narrative, or at least the Matthean account of the incident, was modeled after another one of Daniel's visions, wherein the seer beholds a "**man** clothed in *linen*" with a "face as the appearance of lightning" (Dan. 10:5–6, KJV). In Matthew's version of the Transfiguration, when the disciples hear the voice coming from a "bright cloud" that "overshadowed them," they become terrified and fall on their face to the ground. The transformation of Jesus apparently had no effect on them (Matt. 17:5–6, KJV). Similarly, in Daniel's vision, the men who were with the prophet become terrified and flee, not because they saw the "man clothed in linen," but because his voice sounded like the "voice of a multitude" (Dan. 10:4–7, KJV). Daniel, unlike his companions, does not flee but, instead, falls into a slumber with his "face toward the ground" (Dan. 10:9, KJV), and then, just as Jesus, in the Gospel narrative, touches the disciples that were with him and says, "be not afraid" (Matt. 17:7, KJV), the "man clothed in linen" touches Daniel and says, "Fear not" (Dan. 10:10–12, KJV).

Aside from these striking similarities, however, between the man in Daniel's vision and Matthew's account of the Transfiguration, there is really no reason to believe that the two stories are connected, and with virtually no corroboration from either Mark or Luke the likelihood of any textual relevance seems doubtful.

Perhaps a more germane explanation for the description of Jesus in these Transfiguration narratives lies in other areas of the Bible. The appearance of his face, for example, could be an attempt to connect Jesus with Moses and to rival his relationship with *Yahweh*, the Lord and God of the Israelites. On his second trip up Mount Sinai to meet with "the Lord," Moses was allegedly exposed to the glory of God and, as a result, his face became radiant to the point where he had to wear a veil.[1] For Jesus then to succeed Moses as the new deliverer a comparable event would be needed in order to convince the Jews that he was indeed the Messiah; hence, the whitening of his face during the Transfiguration. This hypothesis could also help explain why Mark does not mention anything about the appearance of Jesus's face in his narration. Since his account of the Transfiguration was from an earlier period than the others, he may not have been as concerned about the opinion of the Jews as Luke and Matthew, or perhaps, at that time, the story had not yet evolved into what it became when Matthew wrote.

The appearance of Jesus in bright white clothing would seem to be symbolic of the purity ascribed to him elsewhere in the Bible[2] as the "unblemished lamb" who gave his life for the atonement of sin. The significance of white in relation to purity is outlined in the book of Revelation, where a multitude of believers who had "washed their robes, and made them white in the blood of the Lamb," are shown to the seer, who identifies himself in the beginning of the apocalypse as John (Rev. 7:9–14, KJV). Also significant is

---

[1]   See Exod. 34.

[2]   2 Cor. 5:21, Heb. 4:15, 1 Pet. 2:22.

the obvious parallel between the Transfiguration of Jesus and the baptismal scene, where God applies his stamp of approval and anoints his "Son."[1]

The anointing of Jesus at the Transfiguration is confirmed by Peter[2] in his second epistle, where it is said that the prophet "received from God the Father honour and glory, when there came such a voice to him from the excellent glory" (2 Peter 1:17, KJV). The fact that Peter, who reportedly witnessed the Transfiguration, refers to God and Jesus as two distinct beings long after the Ascension, while referring only to the "Father" as God, implies that the disciple knew nothing of a divine Messiah. Moreover, the purpose behind the Transfiguration is laid out clearly here by Peter, viz, to bring glory and honor to Jesus. It could not, therefore, have been to reveal his divinity, for if it were the disciple would surely have mentioned something to that effect.

---

[1]   Matt. 3:17, Mark 1:11, and Luke 3:22.

[2]   Or someone writing in his name.

CHAPTER 13

Savior

As we have seen in previous sections, Jesus shares many titles and attributes with the God of Israel in the Christian canon, despite the fact that he is merely a servant of the Almighty, and although these similarities seem to give credence to the "orthodox" view of Jesus, the context of the passages in which these titles appear, more often than not, tells a completely different story. The fact that both God and Jesus are referred to as *savior* in the Christian canon is yet another example of how the early evangelists took the liberty to apply terms and phrases that had been traditionally assigned to *Yahweh* to the one they regarded as lord and master, Son of God, and the long-awaited Messiah, Christ Jesus. This convention, however, warranted or not, in no way justifies the deification of Jesus that began in earnest in the second century of the church and continues to this day, as the role of Jesus in the salvation of Israel and, by extension, "the Greeks," is vastly different from the role of God as the source of all salvation.

To the early evangelists, Jesus was clearly a savior in many respects, but the ultimate savior, by their own admission, was the God and savior who delivered the Children of Israel on numerous occasions from their enemies in the Hebrew scripture. In the Gospel according to Luke, for example, when Mary, the mother of Jesus, learns that she had been chosen to bear the child who would be called "Son of the Most High" (Luke 1:32, ASV) it is the salvation of God that she recalls in the following hymn, which she recites while visiting Elizabeth, the mother of John the Baptist:

> And Mary said, My soul doth magnify the Lord, And my spirit hath rejoiced *in God my Saviour...* For he that is mighty hath done to me great things; And holy is his name... *He hath showed strength with his arm;* He hath scattered the proud in the imagination of their heart. He hath put down princes from their thrones, And hath exalted them of low degree... *He hath given help to Israel* his servant, That he might remember mercy (As he spake unto our fathers) Toward Abraham and his seed for ever. (Luke 1:46–55, ASV)

The "Blessed Mother" undoubtedly knew through divine inspiration that her son was destined to be the Messiah of the Lord as foretold in the scriptures of her ancestors but, at the same time, understood that God, or *Yahweh,* was the one who would actually "help" Israel.

In the same narration, after John the Baptist is born, his father, Zechariah, presents a similar exaltation—supposedly through the Holy Spirit—in which Jesus is referred to as a "horn of salvation" that had been "raised up" by the God of Israel to save them from their enemies in accordance with the scriptures:

> Blessed be the Lord God of Israel; for *he hath visited and redeemed his people,* And hath *raised up an horn of salvation* for us in the house of his servant David; As he spake by the mouth of his holy prophets, which have been since the world began: That we should be saved from our enemies, and from the hand of all that hate us. (Luke 1:68–71, KJV)

As the "horn of salvation" raised up by God, Jesus was expected to deliver his people, but not without the decree from his Lord, and so again we see that the source of salvation in Luke's gospel is *Yahweh*, and it's not until after Jesus is born that the evangelist identifies him as savior:

> And there were in the same country shepherds abiding in the field, keeping watch over their flock by night. And, lo, the angel of the Lord came upon them… And the angel said unto them, Fear not: for, behold, I bring you good tidings of great joy, which shall be to all people. For *unto you is born this day in the city of David a Saviour, which is Christ the Lord.* (Luke 2:8–11, KJV)

Notice here, however, that the shepherds are told only that "a" savior is born and not THE savior, and that this savior is Christ. In this way Luke defines the role of Jesus as *savior* in terms of his status as God's Anointed; and the Messiah, as we have shown previously, is merely a servant of God, who, in the words of Paul, is the "head of Christ" (1 Cor. 11:3).

After the nativity scene, Luke reports that the son of Mary was circumcised and named Jesus (Luke 2:21), a name that, in its Hebrew form, means "*Yahweh* saves," and thus depicts Jesus as a servant through whom God would save his people and confirms the fact that God, or *Yahweh*, is indeed the source of salvation and the one true savior of which Isaiah reportedly spoke:

> I, even I, am the LORD; and beside me there
> is no saviour. (Isa. 43:11, KJV)

In his second book, Acts of the Apostles, Luke narrates a dialog between Peter and his accusers, wherein the disciple clearly states that Jesus was appointed into the role of Savior by God:[1]

> The God of our fathers raised up Jesus, whom
> ye slew and hanged on a tree. Him hath God
> exalted with his right hand to be a *Prince and
> a Saviour*, for to give repentance to Israel, and
> forgiveness of sins. (Acts 5:30–31, KJV)

As "Prince and Savior" Jesus could hardly be considered divine, and, in fact, these words are nearly identical to the words used by Stephen later in the book to describe Moses:

> This Moses whom they refused, saying, Who
> made thee a ruler and a judge? the same did
> God send to be a *ruler and a deliverer* by
> the hand of the angel which appeared to
> him in the bush. He brought them out, after
> that he had shewed wonders and signs in the
> land of Egypt, and in the Red sea, and in the
> wilderness forty years. (Acts 7:35–36, KJV)

---

[1] See also Acts 13:23.

Jesus, therefore, like Moses before him, was merely a servant of God, and both were regarded by the early evangelists as saviors or deliverers.

After the death of Moses it is reported in the Old Testament that God continued to send *saviors* to the children of Israel as long as they repented and returned to the Lord (*Yahweh*). In the time of Judges there was Othniel, son of Kenaz (Judg. 3:7–11); Shamgar, son of Anath (Judg. 3:31); Tola, son of Puah (Judg. 10:1); and Gideon (Judg. 6:36–38). And when the descendents of Jacob desired a king, God sent Saul (1 Sam. 11) and David (2 Sam. 3:17–18) to deliver them from their enemies. In all of these verses the Hebrew word *yasha*, which means to save, is applied to these noble men in the same context it would be later used in reference to Jesus.

Jesus, of course, did not provide any physical deliverance during his brief three-year ministry; however, he was expected to do so upon his return. Until that time the Jews were instructed, by Peter (according to Luke), to repent and return to God "that your sins may be blotted out, when the times of refreshing shall come from the presence of the Lord... For Moses truly said unto the fathers, A prophet shall the Lord your God raise up unto you of your brethren, like unto me; him shall ye hear in all things whatsoever he shall say unto you" (Acts 3:19–22, KJV).

Jesus did reportedly heal the sick that had faith in him, but this was done in all likelihood to prove that he was a prophet like Moses,[1] "whom the LORD knew face to face, In all the signs and the wonders, which the LORD sent him to do in the land of Egypt to Pharaoh" (Deut. 34:10–11, KJV). For the early evangelists to convince the Jews that Jesus was the Messiah they had first to convince them that he was on par with Moses. It was not enough to simply be a descendent of David, although both were important.

In his letter to Titus, Paul refers to both God and Jesus as "our Savior" but, like Luke, identifies God as the source of salvation. As the head of the Christian mission in Crete, Titus was instructed by Paul to encourage all of the believers, including slaves, to exhibit good character so that "the word of God be not blasphemed" (Titus 2:5, KJV) and that "they may adorn the doctrine of *God our Saviour* in all things" (Titus 2:10, KJV). *For it is the "grace of God" that "bringeth salvation"* (Titus 2:11, KJV), says Paul, and the believers, he submits, should "live soberly, righteously, and godly" as they wait for "the glorious appearing of *the great God and our Saviour Jesus Christ*; Who gave himself for us, that he might redeem us from all iniquity" (Titus 2:12–14, KJV).

In many versions of the Bible, Jesus is depicted as both the "great God" and the Savior in Titus 2:13, which in *Young's Literal Translation* is rendered: "waiting for the blessed hope and manifestation of… *our great God and Saviour Jesus Christ*." This, however, is more than just a matter of translation; it is a matter of interpretation as well. Regardless

---

[1]   In the Gospel according to John, Jesus says that the miracles he performed "bear witness of me, that the Father hath sent me" (John 5:36, KJV).

of whether or not these alternative translations are valid, it is evident from the context of the passage that Paul did not confuse Jesus with God. As the dialog continues in the following chapter, Paul explains to Titus: "For we ourselves also were sometimes foolish, disobedient… and hating one another. But after that the kindness and love of *God our Saviour* toward man appeared, Not by works of righteousness which we have done, but according to his mercy *he saved us*, by the washing of regeneration, and renewing of the Holy Ghost; Which he shed on us abundantly ***through*** *Jesus Christ our Saviour*" (Titus 3:3–6, KJV). In other words, God is the one who actually saved the believers, by "the washing of regeneration, and renewing of the Holy Ghost," and Jesus was merely an agent through which God would save the believers. Jesus received the Holy Spirit, it was believed, from God and transmitted it to those whom he commissioned to propagate his message of salvation because he was the one anointed in accordance with the scriptures specifically for this task.[1]

According to the narratives of both Mark and Matthew, Jesus needed to be saved just like any other prophet and, like his ancestors before him who relied upon the Lord in times of great distress, called to God for help as he reportedly suffered on the cross: [2]

---

[1]   See Chapter 10 for details pertaining to the "pouring out" of God's spirit in messianic times.

[2]   Matthew 27:46 contains a quote from the beginning of Psalm 22, a lament attributed to David, who often found himself in similar near-death situations; see also Mark 15:34.

> And about the ninth hour Jesus cried with a
> loud voice, saying, Eli, Eli, lama sabachthani?
> that is to say, My God, my God, why hast
> thou forsaken me? (Matt. 27:46, KJV)

As far as the early evangelists knew, Jesus was not spared the agony of death but was revived, or resurrected, by God, before his body would "see corruption":

> Ye men of Israel, hear these words; Jesus of
> Nazareth, a man approved of God among
> you by miracles and wonders and signs,
> which God did by him in the midst of you,
> as ye yourselves also know: Him, being
> delivered by the determinate counsel and
> foreknowledge of God, ye have taken, and
> by wicked hands have crucified and slain:
> Whom God hath raised up, having loosed the
> pains of death: because it was not possible
> that he should be holden of it. For David
> speaketh concerning him, I foresaw the Lord
> always before my face, for he is on my right
> hand, that I should not be moved: Therefore
> did my heart rejoice, and my tongue was
> glad; moreover also my flesh shall rest in
> hope: Because thou wilt not leave my soul
> in hell, neither wilt thou suffer thine Holy
> One to see corruption. (Acts 2:22–27, KJV)

These words, attributed to Peter, seem to suggest that the message of salvation delivered initially by Jesus and then later through his disciples, was intended strictly for the Jews, yet in the Johannine tradition Jesus is identified as "savior of the world":

> We have seen and do testify that the Father
> sent the Son to be the Saviour of the world.
> (1 John 4:14, KJV)

In Luke's narration this apparent conflict is resolved when Peter realizes that God had also granted "repentance unto life" (Acts 11:18, KJV) to the Gentiles,[1] while in the Gospel according to John the matter is addressed when Jesus says to a woman of Samaria: "*salvation is of the Jews. But the hour cometh, and now is, when the true worshippers shall worship the Father in spirit and in truth: for the Father seeketh such to worship him*" (John 4:22–23, KJV).

In the prophetic writings of the Old Testament, the Jews were promised salvation at the end of days, but not at the demise of every nation. According to the book of Isaiah, when the temple of the Lord (*Yahweh*) is finally established as the highest mountain, the people of "the nations" will come to the Jews to learn about God, and no one will fight anyone anymore:

> And it shall come to pass *in the last days,*
> that the mountain of the LORD's house shall
> be established in the top of the mountains,
> and shall be exalted above the hills; and all
> nations shall flow unto it. And *many people
> shall go and say, Come ye, and let us go up
> to the mountain of the LORD, to the house
> of the God of Jacob; and he will teach us
> of his ways*, and we will walk in his paths:
> for out of Zion shall go forth the law, and
> the word of the LORD from Jerusalem. And

---

[1]   See Acts 10:9 thru 11:18.

> he shall judge among the nations, and shall
> rebuke many people: and they shall beat their
> swords into plowshares, and their spears into
> pruninghooks: nation shall not lift up sword
> against nation, neither shall they learn war
> any more. (Isa. 2:2–4, KJV)

The Samaritans apparently were familiar with these prophecies, for when they learn in John's Gospel that Jesus is in fact the Messiah they proclaim: "this is indeed the Christ, the Saviour of the world" (John 4:42, KJV). Having been themselves oppressed, much like their rivals (the Jews), they presumably were excited about the prospect of universal peace.

In the Hebrew scripture, salvation from enemies is often preceded by forgiveness from sin and/or repentance from the Children of Israel,[1] and in the book of Isaiah the Jews are told explicitly that it was because of their sins that God had not delivered them:

> Behold, the LORD's hand is not shortened,
> that it cannot save; neither his ear heavy,
> that it cannot hear: But your iniquities have
> separated between you and your God, and
> your sins have hid his face from you, that he
> will not hear. (Isa. 59:1–2, KJV)

The early evangelists presumably believed that the blood of Christ had atoned for the "sins of the world" and that the Son of Man, upon his return, would restore Israel for good, thereby providing "salvation" for all eternity through the

---

[1]   See Ps. 79:9–10, Ps. 85:1–4, Judg. 3:7–11, Isa. 19:20.

elimination of war. But, Jesus offered his followers salvation from the "second death" that Daniel alluded to at the end of his book (Dan. 12:1–2) and John spoke of frequently in his apocalypse.[1] "For God sent not his Son into the world to condemn the world; but that the world *through him* might be saved" (John 3:17, KJV), says Jesus, in one of the most heavily quoted verses in the Bible, while in a related verse the prophet explains what he meant by this:

> And if any man hear my words, and believe not, I judge him not: for I came not to judge the world, but to save the world. He that rejecteth me, and receiveth not my words, hath one that judgeth him: the word that I have spoken, the same shall judge him in the last day. (John 12:47–48, KJV)

In other words, it was only those who did not observe the words spoken by Jesus that were condemned, and the role of Jesus was merely to deliver these words, so that those who do believe might be saved. During biblical times, God sent many prophets into the world so that the people who followed them would be *saved* from the punishment of Hell *through* the message they delivered and the examples that they set. In fact, "saving the world" was the primary purpose of every prophet. Jesus, however, was more than just an ordinary prophet; he was the long-awaited prophet known as the Messiah, and the Messiah, according to Jewish tradition, was supposed to be a great deliverer. The early evangelists, therefore, understandably referred to their master as Savior, and when they witnessed (or heard about) what was believed

---

[1]   Rev. 2:11, Rev. 20:6, Rev. 20:14, Rev. 21:8.

to be his death and resurrection they had no choice but to look into the scriptures for answers,[1] and, as a result, we have today the doctrine of vicarious atonement as the cornerstone of the Christian faith, which transformed Jesus from a false prophet[2] into a sacrificial lamb, who was exalted into heaven until a time appointed for him to return and establish his kingdom.

Even this remarkable feat, however, did not engender anything near the level of praise that led to the deification of Christ in the years that followed. The early evangelists demonstrated throughout the Christian canon their belief that God and Jesus were two distinct and completely disparate beings, and to think that they would even entertain the idea that Jesus was God is unfathomable, given the fact (or assumption) that they were either Jews themselves or gentiles closely connected with the Jewish community, because nowhere in the Hebrew Bible is the incarnation of God foretold. It was the "Son of God," we are told, who was crucified and buried,[3] and the Son of God, according to the authors of the Bible, was a man anointed by God to serve him and obey him.[4] How then could he be God?

---

[1]   There is reason to believe, from the text of the Bible, that the disciples of Jesus did not expect to see their master crucified (See Luke 24:13-27) and that the Jews did not anticipate a suffering Messiah (See Acts 17:1-3)

[2]   According to Paul's interpretation of Deuteronomy 21:22–23, Jesus became a cursed man when he was allegedly crucified (See Gal. 3:13).

[3]   Matt. 27:39–40 and 27:54, Mark 14:60–64, John 20:30–31.

[4]   John 15:10, 2 Sam. 7:8–17, Matt. 4:1–11, and Acts 2:22.

CONCLUSION

Although the nature of Jesus and the nature of his mission were undoubtedly regarded with the utmost importance by the early evangelists, it is clear from the manuscripts they left behind that obedience to God and the obtainment of HIS salvation were at the forefront of their discussions, just as in the Hebrew Bible it is the redemption of Israel and their adherence to the law that reigns paramount. Thus, even as Jesus is exalted above the rest of mankind repeatedly in the Christian canon, he remains human and subordinate to God from the infancy narratives to the apocalypse of John and the final judgment. It cannot be denied that Abraham, Moses, and all the prophets of the Old Testament held firmly to the belief in one universal and supreme deity, and so it's only logical to think that the authors of the New Testament, who based their testimony on these scriptures, were equally unitarian in their perception of God.

In our discussion we have attempted to touch on all the major titles, expressions, and attributes associated with Jesus in the Bible and to contrast the church's interpretation of these verses with the contextual meaning derived from the corresponding passages, highlighting differences between the traditional view of Jesus and the written testimony of the early evangelists, and how the Islamic view of Jesus is actually more in-line with the biblical text than the orthodox teachings of Christianity. It is not, however, the intent of the author to ridicule or chastise anyone for practicing Christianity. In the words of Allah, Christians are "the closest in affection to the believers (i.e., Muslims)"[1] and for aspiring to the principles of morality exemplified by Christ they should be commended. The point is that the integrity of the Bible has been corrupted, as attested to by Christian scholars, and the message of Jesus, therefore, distorted; and so it is only in the Koran and the teachings of Prophet Muhammad that the true meaning of monotheism and the unity of God can be found.

It should also be noted that Islam does not demand from the Christian that he/she discard his/her faith entirely. Both Jews and Christians are encouraged in the Koran to build upon the faith they already have and to correct any misunderstandings they may have regarding the unity of God and the prophethood of Jesus, which are both outlined clearly in the Koran. To be a Muslim one simply needs to testify that there are no gods or deities worthy of worship except the one true God—the God of Abraham, Moses, and Jesus—and that Muhammad (Peace be upon him) is the final messenger of God.

The idea that Muhammad could have been a prophet is understandably a difficult pill to swallow for most Christians, particularly those who have never lived in a

---

[1]   Al-Ma'idah:82.

nation or community where Islam is prevalent; and since the advent of the Messiah, according to orthodox Christianity, marked the beginning of a new age in which everything that was foretold would eventually be fulfilled through either Christ himself or the members of his church, there doesn't seem to be any reason for the Christian to embrace the prophet of Islam. When one considers, however, the multitude of people, both men and women, who have reportedly communicated with God in the Old Testament, it seems illogical to dismiss Muhammad, whose prophethood is completely verifiable and practically irrefutable, while accepting every prophet, seer, and man of God recorded in the Bible based on little more than oral tradition.

The miracles that were performed by the likes of Moses, Elijah, and Jesus were undoubtedly convincing to the people who were there to behold them, but to believe in these stories today requires faith and reliance on tradition. Similarly, in the case of Muhammad, there were miracles he performed[1] that can only be acknowledged through the testimony of those who witnessed them, but the miracle of the Koran is available for all generations—past, present and future—to verify and to witness firsthand the veracity of Muhammad's claim that he was a mercy to mankind and the seal of the prophets.

As history shows, the people of Arabia, under the leadership of Muhammad and the guidance of the Koran, were transformed

---

[1]   Among the miracles that Muhammad performed are the splitting of the moon, providing an abundance of water through his hands/fingers, and making it rain when no clouds were visible.

from a backward, pagan, and impoverished nation into a thriving and upright monotheistic community that became the center of civilization.[1] To think that Muhammad, an uneducated, insignificant, and moderately successful merchant, could have accomplished this monumental task—which has affected countless lives until today and changed the course of history forever—without some sort of guidance from above is untenable. Indeed it was the precepts, principals and wisdom of the Koran that enabled the early Muslims to excel as a nation in so many aspects of life, including science, education, civil liberties, social justice, and the arts.

The depth of the Koran, its ever-relevant wealth of information, the preciseness and perfection with which it describes the activities of past generations, the fate of future generations, the purpose of nature, and the meaning of life, combined with its elegant wording, unique style, evident truths, and convincing arguments, leave the unbiased reader with no choice but to acknowledge it as the word of God, and the skeptic yearning for an alternative explanation.

Interestingly enough, the only plausible explanation that the critics of Islam have been able to come up with in the fourteen centuries since the Koran was revealed is that the prophet of Islam modeled his book after certain portions of the Bible—a convincing argument, no doubt, however, one that fails to account for the fact that the Koran is

---

[1]   At the height of the Islamic state, when the rest of Europe was going through its "Dark Ages," Spain remained a thriving community under Muslim rule, to which people would flock from surrounding areas for education, protection, and prosperity.

flawless while the Bible is not, the fact that Muhammad was illiterate, or the fact that the messenger of Allah was notorious for his honesty.

In the Bible there are numerous contradictions and inconsistencies[1] due to the fact that it was written and/or edited by a variety of different people over an unknown span of time. If Muhammad, therefore, was using the Bible as a reference, how is it that we do not find any such discrepancies contained within the Koran, which was compiled over a period of twenty-three years? How was the Prophet able to remain consistent with his message for such a long period of time?

The story of creation in the book of Genesis reveals that the author's knowledge of the earth and its relationship with the sun is consistent with the knowledge of the people at the time it was composed, which is not exactly known, although it is obvious it was written at a time when the earth was believed to be the center of the universe because the earth, according to the Bible, was created before the sun.[2] Today we know that this is not the case and that the earth is part of a complex solar system, but Muhammad, an illiterate man living in the seventh century of the Christian era, would not likely have known about the earth's rotation around the sun; yet he was somehow able to avoid the mistake of the Bible when relating the story of creation in the Koran.[3]

---

[1]   Compare Matthew's genealogy of Jesus (Matt. 1:1–17) to that of Luke's (Luke 3:23–38), or Matthew's list of the disciples (Matt. 10:2–4) to that of Luke's (Luke 6:13–16).

[2]   See Gen. 1:1–23.

[3]   See chapters 10:3, 11:7, 25:59, 32:4, 41:10, 50:38, and 57:4 in the Holy Koran.

In the Gospel according to Matthew, Jesus reportedly tells his disciples: "There be some standing here, which shall not taste of death, till they see the Son of man **coming** in his kingdom" (Matt. 16:28, KJV). Now here it is, some two thousand years later, and the Son of Man has yet to **come** and establish his kingdom, and the disciples undoubtedly have all since perished. The Koran, by comparison, contains prophecies that have indeed been fulfilled and are easily verifiable without the need for the twisting of words or testimony from sources of questionable authenticity. Sometime after the ascension of Heraclius in 610 CE, for example, when the Byzantines (formerly part of the greater Roman Empire) had suffered a major defeat at the hands of the Persians, the following verses were revealed to Muhammad that predicted a subsequent victory for the Romans to the north of Arabia:

> The Romans have been defeated in the nearest land, but they, after their defeat, will overcome within a few years. (Ar-Rum:2–4)

By 630 CE, Heraclius had defeated the Persians on several fronts and regained control of Jerusalem, just as Allah had stated in his revelation to Muhammad, and so it is evident from this and other verses like it[1] that the Koran is the immutable and unmitigated word of God, the All-Knowing,

---

[1]   In *Surah* (chapter) 111 of the Koran, Allah condemns Abu Lahab, (the nickname for) an uncle of Muhammad's, who was a staunch adversary of the Prophet and the message of Islam. He could have easily disproved the Koran and discreditted his nephew by simply accepting Islam. Instead, he died a disbeliever, just as the Koran had predicted.

All-Seeing, who has revealed to his prophet signs of his existence for all mankind to see in a book of guidance that clearly differentiates truth from falsehood.

If Muhammad was lying about the origin of the Koran, then presumably he did so in order to achieve a position of authority, which he eventually did, but even as the head of his newly formed state the Prophet continued to endure hardships and did not indulge in the pleasures of this world. He could have had all the wealth and power he desired without going through the struggles that he did had he been willing to stop preaching the message of Islam, but it was neither wealth nor power that the Messenger of Allah was seeking. When the leaders of Quraish, the dominant tribe of Mecca, sensed that the migration of people away from the worship of their idols would have an adverse effect on their trade, they offered to make Muhammad their king, if only he would denounce the "new religion" (as they saw it). The Prophet refused their offer and died a poor man, monetarily speaking, affirming his sincerity and attesting to the pure, selfless nature of his intentions.

With all the evidence in support of Muhammad and the divine origin of the Koran, is it any wonder why so many people have accepted Islam since the time of the Prophet and that Islam remains the fastest-growing religion in the world today? The peace of mind that one enjoys knowing for certain that he or she is on the straight path that leads to salvation, together with the fairness and justice that Islam promotes, has attracted countless souls to this peaceful way of life.

It is not the will of Allah, however, that all of humanity be guided to Islam. Both the Koran and the Bible concur that there will be some who disbelieve in the word of Allah (God). In the end it is up to each and every one of us to decide for ourselves which path to follow as we wait to meet our Lord, and when that day comes we will all have to face the consequences of our decision. In the meantime, let us remain vigilant in our pursuit of the truth and ask the Almighty for guidance, for without his help we would all be lost, as Allah says in the Koran:

> By the passage of time (Allah swears). Indeed mankind is in loss. Except those who believe and do righteous deeds and encourage others to the truth and encourage others to be patient. (Al-'Asr:1–3)

APPENDIX A: THE KORAN AND MODERN SCIENCE

In 1929, when an American astronomer named Edwin Hubble discovered that all of the stars in all of the galaxies are steadily moving away from each other, scientists later concluded that the universe in its entirety must have originated from a single point that apparently exploded and has been expanding ever since. Today this hypothesis, known as the big bang theory, has become widely accepted and is generally regarded as the only viable explanation for the apparition observed by Mr. Hubble.

For Prophet Muhammad, an illiterate man living in one of the most impoverished and backward regions of the world in the seventh century of the Christian era, to know anything about the expanding nature of our universe would be amazing, to say the least, and flat-out impossible from a statistical standpoint. Yet, this is precisely what is implied by those who deny the divine origin of the Koran, because in the Koran this vital concept of modern astronomy is described vividly in no uncertain terms:

> Have not those who disbelieve known that
> the heavens and the earth were joined
> together as one united piece, and then we
> parted them? (Al-Anbiya':30)

> It is we who have built the universe with
> power and, verily, it is we who are steadily
> expanding it. (Adh-Dhariyat:47)

In the field of biology it is a well-known and established fact that water is the basic building block of life and that all life forms, whether part of the plant kingdom or animal kingdom, rely on this basic molecule for their very survival. Although not necessarily a recent discovery, the likelihood of Muhammad obtaining access to this knowledge, or anyone else, for that matter, living in the seventh century of the Christian era—approximately one full millennium before the discovery of living cells—seems staggering. Yet, this fundamental reality of natural science is stated plainly in the book that the Prophet is given credit for producing:

> And we have made from water every
> living thing. Will they not then believe?
> (Al-Anbiya':30)

When Prophet Muhammad began delivering the message of the Koran to his people one of the concepts they found most difficult to accept is the fact that all of their bodies would one day be resurrected, and so to confront this understandable yet faulty way of thinking, the author of the Koran assures them (and us) in numerous verses that they will indeed be resurrected and presents tangible evidence, or signs, for all of us to contemplate, such as the formation of a child in the womb of its mother and the return to life of a barren land after a rain descends upon it:

> O People, if you should be in doubt about the Resurrection, then [consider that] indeed, We created you from dust, then from a sperm-drop, then *from a clinging clot (alaqah), and then from a lump of flesh (mudghah)*, formed and unformed—that We may show you. And We settle in the wombs whom We will for a specified term, then We bring you out as a child, and then [We develop you] that you may reach your [time of] maturity. And among you is he who is taken in [early] death, and among you is he who is returned to the most decrepit [old] age so that he knows, after [once having] knowledge, nothing. And you see the earth barren, but when We send down upon it rain, it quivers and swells and grows [something] of every beautiful kind. (Al-Hajj:5)

At the time of Muhammad there was no such thing as embryology, and virtually nothing was known about the stages of embryonic development. Yet, amazingly, the manner in which the Koran describes the formation of life in the womb of a mother-to-be is in perfect harmony with the knowledge of embryology obtained through years of modern research.

The Arabic word *alaqah*, for example, translated here as a "clinging clot," provides a remarkably accurate description of the embryo in its earliest stage of development because it is in this stage that the embryo attaches itself or, in other words, "clings" to the wall of its mother's uterus. It is also in this stage that the embryo begins to receive nourishment through the blood of its mother, which coincides with another meaning derived from the word *alaqah*, "leech."

At some point, according to the Koran, the *alaqah* becomes a *mudghah,* or "lump of flesh," *mukhallaqatin wa ghayri mukhallaqatin* (formed and unformed), which alludes to the fact that, as the developing embryo begins to grow and take form, it continues to appear as a tiny mass of flesh, and it was only through advanced technology and the development of high-powered microscopes that scientists have been able to detect the formation of the head and spine during this stage.

BIBLIOGRAPHY

Abdul-Ahad, Dawud. *Muhammad in the Bible.* Malaysia: Pustaka Antara, 1979.

Al-Ansari, Muhammad. *Islam and Christianity in the Modern World.* Karachi: Trade & Industry Publications, 1976.

Ali, Muhammad Mohar. *A Word of Word Meaning of the Qur'an.* Ipswich: Jam'iyat Ihyaa' Minhaaj Al-Sunnah, 2003.

Badawi, Jamal. *Series of Interviews with Dr. Jamal A. Badawi.* Islamic Information Foundation.

Bucaille, Maurice. *The Bible, the Quran & Modern Science.* Paris: Seghers, 1982.

Deedat, Ahmed. *The Choice, Islam and Christianity,* Vol. 1. Saudi Arabia: Fahil Khair, 1994.

———. *The Choice, Islam and Christianity,* Vol. 2. New York: Sanatech Printing.

Friedman, Richard Elliott. *The Bible with Sources Revealed.* New York: HarperCollins, 2003.

Global Encyclopedia. Alexandria: Global Industries, 1987.

Holy Bible. King James Version (public domain).

Holy Bible. American Standard Version (public domain).

Holy Bible. Young's Literal Translation (public domain).

Holy Bible. New International Version. Grand Rapids: Zondervan, 1984.

Holy Bible. Holman Christian Standard Bible. Nashville: Holman Bible Publishers, 2003.

Ibn Kathir. *The Signs before the Day of Judgment*. London: Dar Al Taqwa, 1994.

Ibrahim, I. A. *A Brief Illustrated Guide to Understanding Islam*. Houston: Darussalam, 1997.

New American Bible. Iowa Falls: World Bible Publishers, 1991.

Philips, Bilal. *The True Message of Jesus Christ*. UAE: Dar Al Fatah, 1996.

Qutb, Sayyid. *In the Shade of the Qur'an*. UK: The Islamic Foundation, 1999.

Ridge, Mian. *Jesus: The Unauthorized Version*. New York: Penguin (USA), 2006.

The New Strong's Concise Concordance & Vine's Concise Dictionary of the Bible. Nashville: Thomas Nelson, 1999.

Syed, Ashfaque Ullah. *Index of Qur'anic Topics.* Washington: Amana Publications, 1998.

The Torah, A Modern Commentary. New York: Union of American Hebrew Congregations, 1981.

Wills, Gary. *What Paul Meant.* New York: Penguin (USA), 2006.

Yahya, Harun. *Some Secrets of the Qur'an.* Turkey: Global Publishing, 2001.

_____. *Allah Is Known through Reason.* New Delhi: Goodword Books, 2000.